Corner House Publishers

SOCIAL SCIENCE REPRINTS

General Editor MAURICE FILLER

THE AMERICAN SLAVE-TRADE

KIDNAPPING BEN JOHNSON BECAME A SLAVE HIMSELF.

See page 54.

THE AMERICAN SLAVE-TRADE

AN ACCOUNT OF

ITS ORIGIN, GROWTH AND SUPPRESSION

BY

JOHN R. SPEARS

ILLUSTRATED BY

WALTER APPLETON CLARK

CORNER HOUSE PUBLISHERS
WILLIAMSTOWN, MASSACHUSETTS 01267
1978

Copyright, 1900, by

CHARLES SCRIBNER'S SONS

REPRINTED 1970

BY

CORNER HOUSE PUBLISHERS

Second Impression 1978

LIBRARY OF CONGRESS CATALOG CARD NUMBER: 79-136150

0-87928-009-3

Printed in the United States of America

PREFACE

THIS history of the American slave-trade grew out of a study of the history of the American navy. The navy was in a way connected with the slave-trade, but the subject was so large that only the briefest mention of what the navy did on the slave coast could be made in "The History of Our Navy." The discovery that our naval ships, in forces ranging from a single schooner to a frigate squadron, had cruised on the coast of Africa at intervals during a period of nearly forty years for the proclaimed purpose of suppressing the slave-trade without accomplishing so much as a restriction of it, determined me to give the subject a separate consideration. What I have gathered I have set down here as well as I could.

As it seems to me, the facts form the most remarkable story known to the history of commercial enterprises. Consider, for instance, the origin of the trade. It was established because of the sincere pity of a tender-hearted and most praiseworthy priest for an outraged people. No other trade ever had such an exalted origin, and yet the cruelties and horrors of it far surpass those described in any other branch of history. The soldiers who have looted cities, the

pirates who have made passengers and sailors walk
the plank, and the religious zealots who have burned
their opponents at the stake, were more merciful than
the slave-traders.

Further than that, no trade ever paid such large
returns on the investments. More remarkable still,
the trade at one time made some who followed it
heroes, but at last degraded all who were connected
with it beyond the power of words to describe.

But now that I have written out the facts, I am
bound to say, here in advance, and to repeat further
on, that the intrinsic evil in the slave-trade was not
found in the slaughter of the helpless during the
raids in Africa, or the horrors of the middle passage,
or the brutality of planters who deliberately worked
their slaves to death as a matter of business policy ;
nor was it in all of these combined. I cannot say all
that is in my thought, but it is a fact that the slave
trade and the plantations *might* have been carried on
profitably without any cruelty whatever to the slave.
It is a matter of knowledge among people now living
that many planters promoted the physical comforts
and added to the mental pleasures of their slaves,
while here and there a ship was found to make the
middle passage without losing a life. The horrors of
the trade that cried aloud to heaven for more than
three hundred years were merely the grosser natural
outgrowths of the root evil in it.

Nor is that all. If we look at the story with judicial mind (and it is necessary, though difficult, to do
so) we shall find that the ills brought upon the domi-

nant race by the slave-trade and slavery are more to
be deplored than those inflicted upon the manifestly
oppressed negro.

At first thought it may seem a story to make an
American ashamed of his country. Certainly the
power of the slave-ship owner in national politics
before the civil war was something that makes us mar-
vel now. From the enactment of the law that made
the slave-trade piracy until Abraham Lincoln became
President the policy of pretence that prevailed in
connection with the slave-trade was infinitely dis-
graceful to the nation. But when all the facts are
fairly considered, it is found that we were steadily
developing, under adverse circumstances, a love of
exact Justice. We washed away our shame, at last,
with unstinted blood, and then a time came when our
people took up arms to give liberty even to an alien
race. The history of the slaver days is worth consideration if only that it may be contrasted with the
history of the end of the Nineteenth Century.

This book has been written almost wholly from
public documents, biographies, stories of travellers,
and other sources of original information. I am under
especial obligations to the work of Professor Du Bois
on the suppression of the slave-trade for its full lists
of references, and to Mr. A. S. Clark, without whose
knowledge of the book trade I should have been
unable to complete my collection of authorities.

J. R. S.

CONTENTS

CHAPTER I

THE TRADE IN THE EARLIEST DAYS

CHAPTER II

OLD-TIME SLAVER CAPTAINS AND THEIR SHIPS

CHAPTER III

WHEN VOYAGES WENT AWRY

xi

CHAPTER IV

THE SLAVER AND HER OUTFIT

CHAPTER V

ON THE SLAVE-COAST

CHAPTER VI

THE MIDDLE PASSAGE

CHAPTER VII

THE SLAVERS' PROFIT

CHAPTER VIII

SLAVER LEGISLATION IN THE AMERICAN COLONIES

CHAPTER IX

THE EARLY WORK FOR EXTIRPATION

CHAPTER X

THE SLAVERS OUTLAWED

CHAPTER XI

TALES OF THE EARLIER SMUGGLERS

CHAPTER XII

SLAVERS DECLARED PIRATES

CHAPTER XIII

INTERNATIONAL CO-OPERATION FOR SUPPRESSING THE TRADE

CHAPTER XIV

TALES OF THE OUTLAWED TRADE

CHAPTER XV

THE NAVY AND THE SLAVE-TRADE

Story of the Half-hearted, Wholly Futile Work of Blockading the African Coast—Reward of an Officer Who Earnestly Strove to Stop the Trade—An Interesting Period in the Career of Commodore M. C. Perry—American and British Squadrons Compared—The Sham Work of the Buchanan Administration,

CHAPTER XVI

FREE-NEGRO COLONIES AND THE SLAVE-TRADE

England Led the Way by Establishing a Colony at Sierra Leone to Provide a Home for Negroes Carried from the United States during the Revolutionary War—The Enterprise Saved by the Sturdy Maroons—Origin of the American Society for Colonizing Free People of Color—Life of the Colonists at Cape Mesurado—The Nation of Liberia Organized—An Ape of Philanthropy,

CHAPTER XVII

TALES OF THE COASTWISE SLAVE-SHIPS

Colored Men from New York Prison Sent to New Orleans and Sold—Stealing Slaves in New Jersey for the Southwest Market—Coastwise Slavers that Lost their Human Cargoes in British Islands—Madison Washington a Negro Worthy of his Name—Joshua R. Giddings and the Coastwise Trade—Extent of the Coastwise Traffic,

CHAPTER XVIII

STORY OF THE AMISTAD

A Cuban Coastwise Slaver that may have been Used to Smuggle Slaves Into the United States—On the Way from Havana to Puerto Principe the Slaves Overpowered the Crew, and Started Back to Africa, but were Beguiled to Long Island—Judicially Decided that Slaves Unlawfully Held have a Right to Take Human Life in a Stroke for Liberty,

CHAPTER XIX

LATTER-DAY SLAVE SMUGGLERS

CHAPTER XX

WHEN THE END CAME

ILLUSTRATIONS

CHAPTER I

THE TRADE IN THE EARLIEST DAYS

The Unnamed Dutch Slaver of 1619—First Slaver Fitted Out in American Waters and the First American-built Slaver—When Human Beings were Frequently a Part of a Ship's General Cargo—How a Good Priest, through a Love of Humanity, Promoted the Traffic—Days when Christian Missionaries Found Profit in the Trade, and It Hurt the Conscience of No One Engaged in It—Kings and Nobles as Slave-Traders—A Slaver Contract that was Considered a Magnificent Triumph of Diplomacy—The Yankee Slavers' Successful Stroke for Free Trade and Sailors' Rights—Extent of the Early Traffic.

On a hot day late in the month of August, 1619, while the people of the little British settlement called Jamestown, in what is now the State of Virginia, were busily engaged in the work of establishing homes on the borders of the great American wilderness, an alarm was raised that a ship was coming with the tide up from the sea. Only one more startling cry than that could have been heard—a warning that hostile Indians were coming ; but in those days, when the fighting between nations nominally at peace might cost more lives than were lost in our war with Spain, the approach of an unknown ship, to a settlement as weak as Jamestown, was a most serious matter. It was the more serious for the reason that Spain, in

1

those days, laid claim to all of North America, and was threatening to come to the Chesapeake Bay and lay waste the settlement there as an encroachment upon her rights.

The stranger was a queer-looking craft, if we may judge her by modern standards, for she was, as all ships then were, short and thick—bluff-bowed and round at the stern—while she towered so high out of water at each end that the term "forecastle," which was then and is now applied to any structure at the bow of a ship, was a word of obvious significance. There was literally a castle on her bow, and another, called a poop, on her stern. Her sails, too, of which she carried, doubtless, two on the fore and the main masts, and one on the mizzen, were like great bags bellying out before the wind. When compared with the flat canvas of a modern ship it is easy to see that one would have difficulty in securing a crew for such a ship in these days. But more interesting than the form of either hull or sail was the row of black-muzzled cannon that projected through the bulwarks on each side ; and altogether it is not mere fancy to say that the alarm of such a ship approaching Jamestown carried tremors of fear to the breasts of the weak, and added throbs to the hearts of the strong as they hurried to get their weapons and go down to the river bank to receive her.

But as the stranger drew near, the trained eyes of the colonists saw many signs to allay their fears. She was flying the Dutch flag, for one thing, and the Dutch were then the leading traders of the world. Moreover, it was apparent that her cannon were neither manned nor cast loose for action ; the attitudes and the work of her crew told convincingly that trade, and not war, was wanted, and, seeing this, the ready muskets of the colonists were laid aside that a friendly welcome might be extended.

Then came the ship to the shore, where her lines were made fast to the near-by trees, and her captain walked over a gang-plank to greet the colonists under the wide-spread, thick-leaved branches, and tell them that he had brought merchandise to exchange for the products of the settlement.

Few more interesting ships than this are known to the history of America. The *Mayflower* only, of all the ships that followed Columbus, may be compared to her, and that by way of contrast, because the New England ship came with men who sought a form of liberty, while the Dutchman came to introduce a kind of slavery. Among the articles of merchandise that the Dutch captain had to offer the colonists were twenty human beings, negroes brought from the coast of Africa, and his ship was probably the first slave-trader to visit what is now the coast of the United States.

From a sailor's point of view also the story of this slaver is remarkable; in fact, it is one of the most singular stories known to the history of commerce. Thus, we know that she hailed from Flushing, and the number of slaves that she brought. There is no doubt about her shape and rig. We are well enough assured as to where she landed, and we are even justified in saying how she was secured to the river's bank. There is an old record containing the names of some of the slaves she landed. But her name and the name of her commander have been lost beyond recovery. She appears above our horizon like a strange sail at sea, showing unmistakably from our present point of view that something is wrong with her; we pass her close enough at hand to see on her decks men and women in distress whom we are wholly unable to relieve, and then she fades away in the mists astern, and is lost forever.

We are indebted to John Rolfe, the man that married the Indian maiden Pocahontas (and so became the most famous squaw-man in history), for the greater part of what we know about the first slave-trader to visit our shores. Rolfe was in Jamestown when the Dutchman came to Virginia waters, and it is his record that says: "a dutch man of warre that sold us twenty Negars" came to Jamestown late in August, 1619.

In other accounts this ship is called a Dutch trader, instead of a "man of warre," while others still call her a privateer. Taking all the statements together, the truth appears to be that she was built as a cargo carrier, and yet was armed, and had a license permitting her to prey on the commerce of the enemies of Holland. Her chief business was as a trader, but incidentally she was a lawful privateer. At what point in Africa, or how, she obtained the negroes is not known.

The story of how she happened to carry her slaves to Virginia is of especial interest here because it includes that of the first ship fitted in United States territory for the slave trade.

In the year 1619 "the rapacious and unscrupulous" Captain Samuel Argall was ruler of the colony of Virginia. Argall was able, energetic, adroit, and conscienceless. He was what ward politicians would call a "heeler" of the Earl of Warwick, a man at once rich and unscrupulous. Among the Earl's possessions was the ship *Treasurer*, and Argall owned a share of her.

During the year 1619 the *Treasurer* came to Virginia, armed as a privateer, and bearing a commission from the Duke of Savoy permitting her to cruise against the Spaniards. Presumably intending such a cruise, she cleared out for the West Indies, where, as her log-book shows, she fell in with a Dutch letter of marque and told him that slaves were wanted in Virginia.

It is fair to presume that the Dutchman at once headed away for the Chesapeake, because John Pory, secretary of the Virginia colony, in a letter to Sir Dudley Carleton, dated September 13, 1619, mentions "the man-of-war of Flushing," and says: "The occasion of this ship's coming hither was an accidental consortship in the West Indies with the *Treasurer*." He adds that the Dutchman wanted to buy provisions, "of which the master pleaded that his vessel was in dire need."

It is a matter of record that the *Treasurer* also brought negro slaves to Virginia, and a woman called Angela was sold to a Mr. Bennett. A record of her may be found in the census record of Virginia made in 1625, according to Hotten's "Original List of Emigrants, etc."

It is possible that the *Treasurer* returned ahead of the Dutchman; but, because the Dutchman was in need of food, and because John Rolfe speaks of the Dutchman's slaves only, it is fair to infer that the Dutchman came first.

The records tell why the *Treasurer* landed but one slave. Says the "Declaration" of the Virginia Coun-

cil, made in 1623 : "Finding Captain Argall, the set-
ter-of-her-out, departed thence, she withdrew herself
instantly from the new Governor's power, and went to
the Somer Islands, then discharged her booty, which
were a certain number of negroes, all of which, even
those that belonged as shares unto the mariners
(whereof they have not long since complained in
court), were taken and placed on the said Earl's
lands, as belonging to his lordship, and so continue."

It is perhaps worth mentioning that it has been
asserted that the slaves ascribed to the Dutchman
really came from the *Treasurer*, and that the letters
and other Virginia documents relating to the matter
were deliberately false, because the Virginians feared
the Spanish would come to avenge the raids which
the *Treasurer* had made in the West Indies. But a
careful reading of all the available matter on the subject shows no real foundation for the assertion.

As to the *Treasurer's* career, a word more must be
told, because, as has been said, she was the first slaver
fitted out in America. She had visited the coast occa-
sionally as a trader between England and the colonies
since 1613, but had not been in the slave-trade until
1619. In this voyage to the West Indies she was
"manned with the ablest men in the colony" (see
"Declaration" of 1623), but on reaching Bermuda she
was declared to be unseaworthy. Her arms were taken
out of her and she was broken up. The robbing of her
crew was a natural incident of the trade, and in after
years common enough.

One more question as to the first slave-carrying
ships in the American trade remains to be considered
—a question that has been raised in connection with

the Spanish settlement of Florida, and with the Norse discoveries on the New England coast. If it be admitted that Eric the Red landed on the New England coast, then it is probable that he carried a woman slave ashore with him. That the Spaniards had negro slaves in their settlement in Florida is not now disputed. Peter Menendez, who held a commission of the King of Spain for a settlement in Florida, landed at St. Augustine on September 8, 1565. He undoubtedly had negro slaves in his party. If anyone wishes to make an exhaustive study of the matter of the landing of the first slaves in America, he can find nearly all the references to authorities needed in the *Magazine of American History* for November, 1891 ; but the question of interest to the present history is not when the first slaves were brought within the present limits of the United States, but when the first slave-ship came here in the prosecution of its traffic in human beings. Certainly neither the Viking nor the Spaniard came as a slave-merchant.

The first American-built slaver of which there is definite record was the ship *Desire*, a vessel of 120 tons, built at Marblehead, in 1636. It does not appear that she was in the trade to Africa, but Winthrop's Journal has the following under the date of February 26, 1638 :

"Mr. Pierce in the Salem ship, the *Desire*, returned from the West Indies after seven months. He had been at Providence, and brought some cotton and tobacco and negroes, etc., from thence, and salt from Tortugas." To this is added a remark worth considering: "Dry fish and strong liquors are the only commodities for those parts."

Meantime another slave-ship had come to Virginia —the *Fortune*, Captain Grey, of London. While on the coast of Africa she had fallen in with an Angola ship loaded with slaves, and had captured her. The slaves were carried to Virginia and exchanged for eighty-five hogsheads and five butts of tobacco, which were sold in London. This was in 1630.

That the Dutch introduced African slaves as soon as they obtained a foothold in America need not be said to those who are familiar with the history of New York. They tried, at first, after the custom of the times, to enslave the aboriginal inhabitants, but the task was found so harassing and unprofitable that they soon sought supplies of blacks from Africa. In fact enslaving red men led to such trouble that a wall was built across the lower end of Manhattan Island, where Wall street is now found, to keep red lovers of liberty from driving the Dutch slave-catchers over the Battery beach into the bay.

The first formal mention of negro slaves in the Dutch Manhattan documents is found in the thirtieth clause of the Charter of Liberties and Exemptions of 1629. It says: "The company will use their endeavors to supply the colonists with as many blacks as they conveniently can." The New Project of Liberties and Exemptions of a later date says "the Incorporated West India Company shall allot to each Patroon twelve Black men and women out of the prizes in which Negroes shall be found." Unquestionably the first slave-ships in the trade to Manhattan Island were privateers, as the first slaver in Virginia was, or they were men-of-war.

Just when the first slaver reached New York is no-

where stated, but we can prove that it was within a
few years after the first blacks were landed in Virginia. In 1644 Director-General Kieft gave liberty to
a number of slaves who had "served the company
eighteen or nineteen years." That is to say they had
been taken into the company's service in 1625 or
1626.

Of the introduction of negro slaves at other points
along the coast nothing need be said here. It was
in those earliest years a very small trade. There were
no ships engaged in carrying slaves exclusively on the
high seas, so far as the record shows, until about 1630,
when the *Fortune* captured the Angola slaver. The
slaves were merely a part of the "general cargo" of
that day. In 1647 the Dutch on Manhattan Island
wrote of "the slave-trade, that hath lain so long dor-
mant, to the great damage of the company." In 1635
the whole number of slaves imported into Virginia
was but twenty-six. In 1642 only seven were imported,
and in 1649 only seventeen. There is no record of the
total importations, but it is certain that the traffic in
all the colonies combined amounted to only a few
hundred previous to 1650—certainly fewer in number than would have made a single cargo in later
years.

Trivial as were these transactions from a commercial
point of view, the facts are all of importance here, not
only because they belonged to the beginning of the
trade, but because they are helpful to an understanding
of the light in which the colonists saw the trade. Did
the colonists think, as they bargained for the blacks,
that there was the beginning of a "fatal traffic" that
was "imposed upon them from without"—did they

" lay aside scruples against " a traffic in human beings before they exchanged their products for the "twenty Negars " ?

The student who looks to see why this Virginia colony was established may see, first of all, in " The True and Sincere Declaration," published in 1609, what the colonists said was their chief object. It reads : " To preach and baptize into the Christian Religion, and, by the propagation of the Gospell, to recover out of the armes of the Devill, a number of poore and miserable soules wrapt up unto death in almost invincible ignorance ; to endeavour the fulfilling and accomplishment of the number of the elect which shall be gathered out of all corners of the earth and to add our myte to the Treasury of Heaven."

They believed that was their chief object, but we have another view of their habits of thought.

In a letter written by Captain John Smith in 1614 we find the following regarding the sport of fishing in the waters of the colony :

" And is it not pretty sport to pull up twopence, sixpence, and twelvepence, as fast as you can haul and veer a line ? "

One may search the entire literature of that day without finding another sentence so significant of the spirit of the age as well as of the colonists—the spirit that measured even its sport in fishing by counting the market value of each fish taken. In all sincerity they would proclaim that missionary work was the first object in making the settlement ; they did truly wish to add their "myte" to the number of "the elect," but with their missionary purposes there was found a proclaimed and unrepressed determination

to make money. They had religious instructors who
turned from a contemplation of the gold-paved streets
of their heavenly home to talk of pay streaks in the
mines of their wilderness home beyond the sea.
And when they had arrived, they laid out a town site,
boomer fashion, after which there was "no talk, no
hope, no work but dig gold, wash gold, refine gold,
loade gold."

But, alas, the dirt did not pan out. They sent a
cargo of glittering stuff home in the first *Supply*, but
it was worthless, so they turned to "pitch, tar, and
soap ashes" ; also to sassafras, with such vigor that
even the "gentlemen" of the colony went to work with
axes and thereby blistered their soft hands until they
swore wicked oaths "at every other stroke" of their
axes. For this they were publicly punished, so that
they were led to hold their tongues, commonly, whatever their thoughts might be.

But "pitch, tar, and soap ashes" also failed to
make them rich, or even comfortable, and the colony
was at the point of absolute extinction when John
Rolfe, the squaw man, introduced the cultivation of tobacco in 1612. With tobacco came, at last, prosperity,
but only at a terrible price. To grow the crop required
the severest kind of toil, and, what was worse, the work
had to be done under conditions that proved deadly to
the colonists of every class.

With these facts held in mind let us recall the
further fact that the greater part of the chopping and
digging was done by "apprentices"—a real "working
class"—a class of men (afterward women were included) who were brought from their homes in England under contract to serve for a stated number of

years, and were sold to the Virginia planters. The whole colonial labor system was based on the apprentice system, and it is a well-known fact that many men of education and ability came to the colonies as "apprentices," and were sold out as merchandise was.

Even that law of Massachusetts in 1641 so often quoted to prove that the colonists there were opposed to human slavery proves, in fact, that voluntary slavery was common. It says: "There shall never be any bond slavery amongst us, unles it be Lawfull captives, taken in just wars, [or such] as [shall] *willingly sell themselves.*"

Holding in mind these facts, consider next the climate of the tobacco-growing region. The extinction of the colony was at one time threatened. Every immigrant had to endure the "seasoning" fever, and the percentage of deaths was frightful.

In this condition of affairs came a trader who offered to exchange twenty black laborers (who would need no "seasoning") for the products of the land which the colonists had in abundance.

Were men who had never obtained a laborer save by purchase, and men who themselves had voluntarily submitted to being bought and sold, to have their consciences afflicted at the thought of buying these strangers? Such an idea could not enter their heads. The fact is that the English Missionary Society that, in the seventeenth century, supplied all English-American colonies with pious pabulum, owned a plantation in Barbadoes and worked it with slaves, while the great Quaker Fox, after a visit to the West Indies, had nothing to say about the principle involved in the traffic, although he was careful to denounce the cruel treatment of slaves.

One more question in connection with this introduction of negro slaves must be considered briefly. Did it pay? Let the facts answer. The planters in the tobacco, rice, cotton, and sugar regions not only increased in number from year to year, but they built finer houses, bought finer clothes and books, and lived in more expensive fashion from generation to generation.

Thus we read: "Everything is by God's blessing in a good condition; and in consequence of the employment of the negroes, which were from time to time introduced from Angola into Brazil, in planting grain, flour is produced in such quantity that what always used to cost eight or ten guilders still continues to be sold at the rate of six stivers." * Such quotations may be multiplied almost indefinitely. In Georgia, the one colony where no slaves were allowed, in early days, the planters became so eager for them that their regular toast when drinking together was "Here's for the one thing needful!"

In short, to sum up the facts, slaves were introduced into United States territory in answer to a demand for labor. They were purchased by men who were accustomed to the purchase and sale of laborers, and no one's conscience was in any way hurt by the transaction. It was a good business proposition for that day, and for two centuries, at least, thereafter.

As for the early West India traffic, for which but brief space can be allowed, it appears that as early as 1503 negroes were carried to Hayti and put at work

* See Vol. I., 167, New York Colonial Documents.

on the plantations there. Herrera writes of these negroes that they "prospered so much in the colony that
it was the opinion that unless a negro should happen
to be hung he would never die, for as yet none had
been known to perish from infirmity." Here was the
very inception of the American trade. When the
Spaniards tried enslaving the aborigines of the island,
the unfortunate red men withered like green corn
under the hot winds of the unirrigated American
desert. Bartholomew de las Casas, filled with pity for
the dying Indian race, rose up in its defence. Good
people have since been moved to apologize for and explain what this Dominican did, but his acts need no
apology from any man. To save the race unfit for
labor there, the Dominican proposed substituting negroes who were both physically and mentally capable
of enduring even the work of digging gold in the torrid zone under the devil-hearted Spaniards of that day.

Having the true state of affairs placed before him by
the humane Dominican, "in the year 1510 the King of
Spain ordered fifty slaves to be sent to Hispaniola to
work in the gold mines." So says Herrera. That
was the beginning of the systematic importation of
Africans into the Spanish West Indies. On the whole,
the Spanish-American slave-trade was, at its inception,
in the interest of humanity, shocking as that assertion may seem at first glance.

That the trade begun in 1510 did not reach our
shores until 1619 is readily explained by the fact that
our shores were not permanently settled by the whites
until nearly a century after that first slave cargo was
sent out.

Of the Spanish slave-trade in that first century we

Only the Royal company was named in the agreement, but all British traders were to participate in the trade. It was contracted on the part of the Spanish that they would take at least 4,800 negroes a year for thirty years, and that the company might sell as many more as it could for twenty-five years at any Spanish-American port except three. In return for this the company paid 200,000 crowns spot cash, a duty of 33½ crowns on each slave landed, and a quarter of its profits each to the Spanish and the British kings.

This contract is found in Article 16 of the Treaty of Utrecht, which was signed on April 11, 1713. Although England obtained by this treaty the Hudson Bay Territory, Acadia, Newfoundland, and Gibraltar, this slave-trade article "was regarded as one of the greatest triumphs of the pacification of 1713."

At the time of this treaty London and Bristol were the slave-ship ports of England, and Newport was the chief one in America. Liverpool entered the slave trade previous to 1730, with "a single barque of thirty tons."

The vessel had half the capacity of one of the sailing lighters common to New York Harbor. An Erie Canal boat carries two hundred and forty tons. But the little bark was profitable, and the trade grew after 1731 until in 1752 Liverpool had eighty-seven vessels in the trade, Bristol one hundred and fifty-seven, and London one hundred and thirty-five. The Liverpool merchants built such sharp and swift ships for the trade that a special wet dock, that would keep them afloat during ebb tide while in that port, had to be built for them. The present great dock system of Liverpool originated in the needs of the slave-traders.

In those days the ship-chandlers of Liverpool made special displays in their windows of such things as handcuffs, leg-shackles, iron collars, short and long chains, and furnaces and copper kettles designed for slavers' use. The newspapers were full of advertisements of slaves and slaver goods. "The young bloods of the town deemed it fine amusement to circulate handbills in which negro girls were offered for sale." An artist of wide repute—Stothard—painted "The voyage of the *Sable Venus* from Angola to the West Indies." The Merchants' Exchange, or Town Hall, as it was called, was ornamented in a way that was strikingly appropriate, for "between the capitals runs an entablature or fillet, on which are placed in base-relief the busts of blackamoors and elephants, with the teeth of the latter, with such-like emblematical figures representing the African trade and commerce." The merchants of Liverpool needed no Ruskin to suggest "pendant purses" for decorating a frieze, or "pillars broad at the base, for the sticking of bills," when they were building a market-place.

In America the New England colonies took the lead in the slave-trade. Barefooted boys waded through the snow to find berths in the forecastles of the colony ships, and, hard as sailor life was then, they found more comforts afloat than on the farms they left behind. And once afloat the Yankee boy worked his way aft as readily as he climbed the ratlines when ordered to reef topsails.

"At the very birth of foreign commerce from New England ports," says one writer,* "the African slave trade became a regular business." The *Desire*, as already mentioned, was a slaver. "The ships which took cargoes of staves and fish to Madeira and the Canaries were accustomed to touch on the coast of Guinea to trade for negroes, who were carried generally to Barbadoes, or the other English islands of the West Indies."

The Massachusetts statute of 1705, which is curiously enough often quoted as showing that the people there were opposed to the slave-trade, was carefully worded to promote the trade. It did, indeed, lay a tax of four pounds on each negro imported, but "a drawback was allowed upon exportation." "The harbors of New England were thus offered as a free exchange-mart for slavers."

In Rhode Island "Governor Cranston, as early as 1708, reported that between 1698 and 1708 one hundred and three vessels were built in that State, all of which were trading to the West Indies and the Southern colonies. They took out lumber and brought back molasses" in the direct trade, but "in most cases made a slave voyage in between."

According to the "Reminiscences of Samuel Hopkins," Rhode Island had one hundred and fifty vessels in the African slave-trade in 1770. Hopkins wrote in that year saying: "Rhode Island has been more deeply interested in the slave-trade, and has enslaved more Africans than any other colony in New England."

In 1787 he wrote again: "This trade in human

* History of Slavery in Massachusetts, by Geo. H. Moore.

species has been the first wheel of commerce in New-port, on which every other movement in business has depended. That town has been built up, and flourished in times past" on the slave-trade, "and by it [the inhabitants] have gotten most of their wealth and riches."

CHAPTER II

OLD-TIME SLAVER CAPTAINS AND THEIR SHIPS

David Lindsay as a Typical American Slaver of the Eighteenth
Century—With a Rotten Ship that Showed Daylight
Through Her Seams "Al Round Her Bow Under Deck"
He Reached the Slave Coast, Gathered His Cargo in Spite
of Fevers, Deaths in the Crew, and Competition, and Finally
Landed at Barbadoes with "All ın Helth and Fatt"—An
Astrologer's Chart for a Slaver's Voyage—Tales of the
Slaver Vikings of Lıverpool—Debt of Early American
Commerce to the Slave Trade—John Paul Jones a Slaver.

DETAILS of the characters of the men and of the
ships that were engaged in the American slave-trade
during the eighteenth century are lamentably hard to
find in these days, but fortunately such as remain to
us are sufficiently graphic and significant.

For a type of the Yankee slavers of the day we may
very well choose Captain David Lindsay, who hailed
from Newport, R. I., in the middle of the eighteenth
century, when that town was one of the liveliest of
American ports. His story has been preserved in a
considerable number of letters and documents that
were printed in the *American Historical Record* some
years ago.

The earliest mention of Captain Lindsay's existence
is found in a letter that comes literally from the sea—
a letter that is dated "June ye 13 1740 at Sea Latt. 8°

30′ N. Long. 39° 30′ W." It was written by one George
Scott, himself a slaver captain, and it contains a variety of matters of interest to the slave-trade in addition
to the references to Captain Lindsay. It reads as
follows:

"GENTLEMEN :—Meeting with this opportunity I was very
glad to acquaint you of our miserable voyage. We left
Anamaboe ye 8th of May, with most of our people and slaves
sick. We have lost 29 slaves. Our purchase was 129. My
negro Bonner is ded; the slaves we have left is now all recovered. We have five that swell'd and how it will be with
them I can't tell. We have one-third of dry cargo left, and
two hhds. rum. If I had staid there for it and sold I believe
I should have lost all our slaves. I think to proceed to
Antigo and fit ye sloop and take ye other trial on the coast.
It will not do to give up for one bad bout. If I go directly
back I'll sell ye rum for gold, if I gitt but twenty pence for it
before I'll by slaves. The slaves that died, I believe there was
one above twenty-two years old and none under fourteen. I
have sent by Captain Lindsay sixteen ounces of gold, which
is all. I wrote you by Capt. Kinnecutt, who sail'd ye 10th
April. I have repented a hundred times ye bying of them
dry goods. Had we laid out two thousand pound in rum
bread and flour, it would [have] purchased more in value than
all our dry goods. I have paid a good part of the wages.
My serviss to all friends, pray excuse all blunders, for I am
now aboard Capt. Lindsay and in haste to gitt aboard."

Observing, by the way, that Captain Scott was determined to " fit ye sloop and take ye other trial on the
coast "—that he was a man of pluck himself—the references to Lindsay mean much to a sailor.

Scott was more than a month out from the African
coast and yet had covered but thirty degrees of west
longitude. Then along comes a vessel, commanded by

Captain Lindsay, that is also bound west, and immediately Captain Scott not only writes a letter to the owners of his ship, which he gives to Lindsay to carry, but he also entrusts all the gold-dust he had obtained to the same hand.

Manifestly Lindsay must have had a fast ship, and he was a man known to make quicker voyages, at least, than Scott. What is of equal importance, Lindsay must have had a reputation as an honest man. Our introduction to Lindsay, though it comes from an unknown slaver and out of the sea, is decidedly in his favor.

The next reference to Lindsay in these documents is in 1752, when he was in command of the brigantine *Sanderson*, belonging to William Johnson, of Newport, R. I. The register of the vessel has been preserved, and reads in part:

"The Brigantine *Sanderson*, whereof David Lindsay is at present master, being a square stern'd vessel of the burthen of about forty tons, was built at Portsmouth, in the colony aforesaid, in the year Seventeen Hundred and Forty-five, and that this deponent at present is sole owner thereof, and that no Foreigner, directly or indirectly, hath any share or part or interest therein."   WILLIAM JOHNSON.

Not only was she small—there are few, if any, of the Hudson River brick schooners that will not carry more cargo—she was a cheaply built vessel, as appears from another document which shows that during the year she was built she was offered for sale for £450, when the cost of building a first-class ship varied from £24 to £27 per ton register.

Finding no sale for her she was kept going, and in the year 1752, with Lindsay in command, she went to

the West Indies for molasses, whence Lindsay wrote
home that she was "tite as yett." She was probably
still "tite" on her return to Newport, for she was at
once loaded for Africa, where she arrived in due time,
and it is then that we learn what kind of pluck Lindsay had. In a letter dated "Anamaboe 28th Feby
1753" he says:

"GENTLEMEN :—This third of mine to you and now I am to
Lett you know my proceed'gs sense my last, Dated 3d Jany,
& I have Gott 13 or 14 hhds of rum yet Left abord, and God
noes when I shall Gett clear of it. Ye traid is so dull it is
actually a noof to make a man creasey. My cheefe mate after
making four or five Trips in the boat was taken sick & Remains very bad yett : then I sent Mr. Taylor & he Gott not
well & three more of my men has been sick. James Dixon is
not well now and wors than yt have wore out my small cable
also oakam & have been oblige to buy one heare, for I thought
the concequance of yr Intrust on bord this vesiel was Two
great to Rusk without a cable to trust, therefore I begg you
not Blaim me in so doeing. I should be glad I cood come
Rite home with my slaves, for my vesiel will not last to proceed farr. We can see daylight al round her bow under deck.
However I hope She will carry me safe home once more. I
need not inlarge. Heare lyes Captains hamlet, James Jepson,
Carpenter, Butler & Lindsay. Gardner is dun. firginson is
Gon to Leward. All these is Rum Ships. butler is in a brig
with 150 hhds from Barbadoes, belongs to Cape Coast Castle.
I've sent a Small boye to my wife. I conclude with my best
Endeavors for Intrust. Gentlemen, your faithful Servant at
com'md   "DAVID LINDSAY.

"N. B. on the whole, I never had so much Trouble in all
my voiges. I shall rite to barbadoes in a few days."

Mr. Taylor was the second officer. Both first and
second were in their bunks, and three of the men in

BRINGING ONE THAT WAS BOUND AND GAGGED.

See page 52.

the forecastle were sick. Terribly short-handed, with slaves in the hold likely to rise up and strike for freedom in case they learned this fact, and with the probability that others of the crew would take the fever, Captain Lindsay found himself in a serious strait, but, worse than all that, "he could see daylight al round her bow under deck."

And yet Captain Lindsay came up from that fearsome look at the open seams of his vessel and went on loading her for the long voyage across the Atlantic.

If we will but look at the case in the light of that day the courage, the fortitude, of the stout-hearted old skipper was inspiring. Nor shall we fail to observe his thoughtfulness for the wife that would hear of the condition of the rotten ship with quaking fears.

So it is with a feeling of relief, and with increased admiration for his pluck, that we find a letter which shows that he reached Barbadoes safely after a most perilous voyage ; our admiration is all the greater because the perils are described so simply. The letter is as follows :

" BARBADOES, June 17th, N. S. 1753.

" GENTLE'N :—These are to acqt of my arivel heare ye Day before yesterday in 10 weeks from Anamaboe. I met on my passage 22 days of very squally winds & continued Rains, so that it beat my sails alto pieces, soe that I was oblige Several Days to have sails onbent to mend them. The vesiel, Likwise is all open Round her bows under deck. For these Reasons am oblige to enter my vesiel heare and have valued myself on Mr. Elias Meriveal, who is to despatch me in three or four weeks' Time. My slaves is not landed yet : they are 56 in number for owners, all in helth & fatt. I lost one small gall. I've got 40 oz gould dust & eight or nine hundred weight Maligabar pepper for owners.

"Not to Inlarge, shall rite in a day or 2. We are all well
on bord. Mr. Sanford died the 3d day of March, & one John
Wood who went in ye boat with him, died ye 3d of April, at
sea. I left Capt. Hamblet at Cape Coast, sick. His slaves
had rose & they lost the best of what they had. Heare is no
slaves at market now."

The reader who knows the sea will fully appreciate
the condition of that tiny ship during those "22 days
of very squally winds"—the tiny ship that was "open
all Round her bows under deck." For she was short-
handed through deaths and sickness, and yet her
pumps had to be kept going during all that time,
while several days were spent in repairing sails that
the winds had blown to pieces.

Nor does this letter tell us of fortitude alone, for it
is a significant fact that Lindsay "lost one small gall"
only, while all the rest were landed "in helth & fatt."
They had been cared for in kindly fashion. The facts
seems to show that Lindsay was superior to the average
slaver of his day. It was then a lawful trade, and we
have testimony that it was "very genteel." More
important still, it was a trade that, more than all
others, taxed the trading ability, the patience, the skill
as a seaman and the fortitude of the men engaged in
it; also, it was, when successfully carried on, the most
profitable branch of commerce. Naturally the most
capable men of the sea were called to this trade. In
short, Lindsay was a type of the race of Yankee
slaver captains.

With all these facts in mind it is amusing to turn
to one other characteristic of this hard-headed old
slaver. Before starting on this eventful voyage he
must needs consult an astrologer, or conjurer, as the

seers of the time were often called, to learn the day
and hour when the ship must sail in order to have all

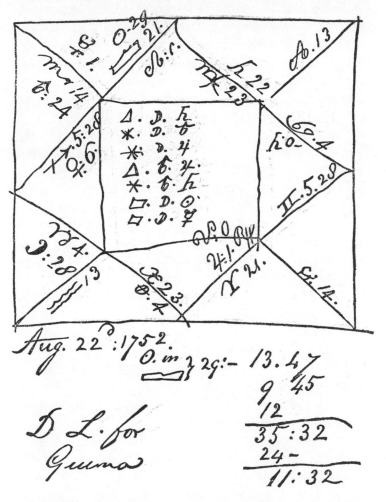

the kindly influences of the heavenly bodies in her
favor. Fortunately the chart which he obtained has
been preserved, and we know from it that "D. L."

sailed "for Guinea at 11.32 o'clock on Aug. 22d, 1752."

Of the English captains engaged in the American trade there was Captain " Billy" Boates, also called "William Boates, Esq., whose extensive transactions in the commercial world rendered him a most useful member of society," to quote an obituary notice of the man from a Liverpool paper. Captain Boates was a waif. His mother or her friends cast him adrift in a Liverpool harbor boat a few hours after his birth. He was picked up, reared in an orphan asylum, apprenticed to a ship master, and then began a career that showed the kind of stock from which he sprang. From the forecastle to the after-cabin required but three steps easily taken. From the cabin to the counting house was a step longer than the three preceding taken together ; but he made the leap.

In the *Knight* he sailed from Anamaboe on January 6, 1758, with three hundred and ninety-eight negroes, of whom, after a voyage that lasted less than six weeks, he landed three hundred and sixty at Jamaica. That was a voyage worth recording for its speed alone ; but off the Leeward Islands the *Knight* fell in with a French privateer that carried " twelve carriage guns and full of men, which attempted to board him several times."

The odds against Captain "Billy" were tremendous, but what he lacked in men and arms he made up by his magnificent pluck. The privateersmen swarmed to his deck, "but never a Dago that got over the rail lived to return."

More famous still as a fighter was Captain Hugh Crow, the one-eyed slaver of Liverpool, "one of the bravest, shrewdest, quaintest and most humorous old sea-dogs that ever breathed" ; but he was of a later date than Lindsay or Boates, being, in fact, captain of the last lawful Liverpool slaver. One would like to tell his whole story, but space can be spared only to say that when in the slaver *Mary* he was attacked at night by two sloops-of-war, each of which was of far superior force. Captain Hugh supposed they were Frenchmen, and, calling his men to quarters, for six hours fought off the determined attacks of both men-o'-war. And then when daylight came he found they were British sloops at that. They had supposed that he was French. All things considered, that was the most splendid battle known to the history of "peaceful commerce."

Indeed as the most important branch of British commerce—the commerce of the new England as well as the old England—the slave-trade became the chief nursery of British seamen. The instincts inherited from viking ancestors were fostered and encouraged there. It must be frankly admitted that not only did the boasted prosperity of both English and American over-sea commerce have its foundation in the slave-trade, but also that the magnificent qualities of the Anglo-Saxon naval seamen of the eighteenth century were nourished in the tiny traders, " of an average of seventy-five tons burthen" from Liverpool, of an average of forty tons from Newport and Boston, that went forth to face the unavoidable hurricanes of the tropical seas and to meet, yardarm to yardarm, the war-ships, privateers, and pirates that were ever on the lookout for such rich prizes as the slavers. The fact is the seamen who manned our ships in the War of the

Revolution, and by their pluck and skill captured the munitions of war that enabled Washington to win at last, were trained on the decks of slavers. And John Paul Jones, one of the " true sea-kings, whose claim to the title lies in the qualities of the head as well as of the heart," came through the forecastle of the slaver *King George* to hoist the first American naval ensign above the quarter-deck of the first American flag-ship.

CHAPTER III

WHEN VOYAGES WENT AWRY

Tales of Trouble When Lying on the Slave Coast—" We are
Ready to Devour One Another, for Our Case is Desprit "—
A Second Mate's Unlucky Trip in a Long Boat—Sickness
in the Hold as Well as Among the Crew—Cocoanuts and
Oranges Could Not Serve in Place of Water—Story of the
Mutiny on the Slaver *Perfect*—Risks the Underwriters As-
sumed—The Proportion of Disastrous Voyages.

" ANAMABOE, October 27th, 1736.

"SIR : After my Respects to you, these may Inform how it
is with me at pres'nt. I bless God I Injoy my health very
well as yett, but am like to have a long and trublesum voyage of it, for there never was so much Rum on the Coast at
one time before. Nor ye like of ye french ships was never
seen before, for ye whole Coast is full of them. for my part
I can give no guess when I shall get away, for I purchest but
27 slaves since I have been here, for slaves is very scarce : we
have had nineteen sails of us at one time in ye Rhoad, so that
those ships that used to carry pryme slaves off is now forsed
to take any that comes : here is 7 sails of us Rum men that we
are ready to devour one another, for our Case is Desprit. Sir,
I beg that you will exist my famely in what they shall want,
for I no not when I shall get home to them myself. I have
had the misfortin to Bury my chefe mate on ye 21st of Sept.
and one man more, and Lost the negro man Prymus and
Adam over board on my pasedge, one three weeks after
another : that makes me now very weke handed for out of
what it left thair is two that is good for nothing. Capt.

31

Hamond has bin heare six months and has but 60 slaves on
bord. My hearty servis to your spouse and famely. I am
y'rs to com'd   " JOHN GRIFFEN."

Before describing fully the evils inflicted on the
slave cargoes it seems but an act of justice to give
here some of the ills endured by the old-time slavers.
We must consider the condition of the conscientious
slaver captain when there were " 7 sails of us Rum
men" in one port anxious to buy slaves—the slaver
captain whose "Case is Desprit"—with such degree
of sympathy as we can summon for his benefit, if we
are to see the trade as it was. Captain Griffen was
one of the Newport slavers. Very likely he was in
the trade when Captain Lindsay was making fame
and wealth; certainly everyone who knows the sea,
and how the time drags while waiting for a cargo in
an unhealthy, unattractive port, far from home, will
sympathize with Captain Hammond, who had been on
the slave-coast for six months and had less than half
a cargo in his hold.

Another letter from the captain, George Scott, already quoted in connection with Captain Lindsay
will show still more clearly how troubles came upon
the slavers. The letter related to the voyage previously mentioned, and it runs as follows :

" ANAMABOE, April ye 9th 1740
"Brother Daniel, this I hope will find you in good health
as I am at present. I have not been very well for five weeks
past, which is made our voyage very backward, and am now
very well recovered, Blessed be God. We have now five
people sick and bonner so bad he will not recover. I am
heartily tired of ye voyage, everything runs so cross that I
undertake to make a voyage. I being not very well, kept my

cheif mate aboard and sent ye second mate in ye Long boat to Leward a trading. He had not been gone above four days before he hired a canoue, sends her up with his gold taken to me for goods, without any orders from me. i sent ye canoue immediately back without goods : going down they overset the canoue, the blacks came off from ye shore and took them up, put them in irons : the blacks where ye [long] boat lay detained ye mate ashore, in which time a man slave he had bought, got out ye boat with two ounces of gold and has got clean off. I was obliged to go down with ye sloop and pay thirty-two pound in ye best of goods before they would let ye mate come off. Upon the hole I've lost nigh three hundred pounds with that trip, in money, by the mate's folly. I am sure he will never be able to make satisfaction.

"I bought some slaves and Goods from a Dutchman for gold, which I thought to sell to ye french, [but] in a little time after [that] my slaves was all taken with the flucks, so that I could not sell them ; lost three with it and have three more very bad : ye rest all well and good slaves. We have now aboard one hundred and no gold. I think to purchase about twenty & go off ye coast : ye time of year don't doe to tarry much longer. Everything of provisions is very dear and scarce : it costs for water Tenn shilling for one day. I think to stay in this place but fourteen days more. We shall go to Shama and water our vessel and sail off ye coast with what I can purchase, which I believe will be 120 slaves cargo. We shall have left about two hundred pound sterg. in goods, which wont sell here to any profitt. Every man slave that we pay all Goods for here, costs twelve pound sterg. prime. I hope I shall be in Barbadoes, ye latter end of June, but have not concluded whither we shall go to Jamaica or Virginia ; our slaves is mostly large. 60 men and men boys, 20 women, the rest boys and girls, but three under four foot high. Pray excuse all blunders and bad writing, for I have not time to coppy, the sloop being under sail."

One of the earliest of the voyages that went awry, of which a record has been preserved, was that of the

Dutch West India Company's ship *St. John*, the log
of which is given in O'Callagan's "Voyages of the
Slavers." The troubles here were due to the parsi-
mony of the owners—rather the directors of the company—who fitted the ship out with rotten food and
water casks that leaked. To take the place of water
they took on 5,000 cocoanuts and 5,000 oranges, but
the slaves died as cattle on the desert do, and at last,
to complete the misery of all, the ship was stranded in
a gale, and then looted by pirates.

Another cause of loss to the slavers was in the mutiny, so-called, of the slaves. Although the negro was
never for a moment to be compared with the North
American Indian as a fighter, he did sometimes, even
as a slave, rise against his oppressor. While the slaver
Perfect, Captain Potter, was at Mana, on January 12,
1759, with nearly one hundred slaves on board, the
captain sent the mate, the second mate, and the boatswain away for slaves that had been paid for. This
expedition took more than half the *Perfect's* crew
away from her; and while they were gone, the slaves
in some way got clear of their manacles and swarmed
up on deck. They killed the captain, the surgeon, the
carpenter, the cooper and a boy, when six other members of the crew got into a boat and fled ashore to the
mate, and thence to the slaver *Spencer*, Captain Daniel
Cooke.

Next morning Captain Cooke took his ship near the
Perfect and "fired his guns into her for about an
hour," but the *Perfect's* mate could not persuade him
to board her. In the end such of the slaves as escaped
the guns of the *Spencer* managed to run the *Perfect*
ashore, where they plundered and burned her.

Of the troubles that came upon the slavers through the wars of the eighteenth century one might write a long and stirring chapter. For the slavers made good fighting, especially when it was viking blood in the slavers against Latin blood in naval ships. But of that nothing can be told here, because the losses were not an outgrowth of the slave-trade as a special branch of commerce. But something may be told of the proportion of losing to paying voyages, even though no list of slavers has been or can be made. In the old papers already mentioned in connection with Captain Lindsay, we find the charges of underwriters set forth, and no better comment on the risks of a trade can be found than an insurance policy. A paragraph from such a policy reads:

" And touching the adventures and perils which we, the assurers are content to bear, and do take upon us in this voyage, they are of the seas, men of War, Fire, Enemies, Pyrates, Rovers, Thieves, Jettisons, Letters of Mart, and Countermart, Sarprizals, Taking at sea, Baratry of the Master, and Marines, and all the Perils, Losses, and Misfortunes that have or shall come to the hurt, Detriment or Damage of the said Goods and Merchandize, or of the said vessel, her Tackel, Apparel and Furniture, or any part thereof."

For assuming these risks the underwriters charged usually £20 in a hundred, but Mr. William Johnson got at least one policy of a hundred for £18 premium.

CHAPTER IV

THE SLAVER AND HER OUTFIT

There were Tiny Ships in the Trade—One Vessel had a Capacity of 5,000 Gallons of Molasses Only, and Even Open Row-Boats were used in the Nineteenth Century—Dimensions of a Slaver's Timbers—The Famous *Venus*, a Forerunner of the Yankee Clippers—Steamers that were in the Trade—The Blubber Kettles of Whalers used for Boiling Rice and Yams—Rum, Guns, and Coin were the Favorite Articles of Traffic, but Silks, Laces, Parasols and Other Goods for the Use of Women of Education and Delicate Tastes were Wanted—A Naval Officer's Estimate for a Slaver's Outfit.

THE *Desire*, built at Marblehead, in 1636, was the earliest American slaver of which we have the size, and she, as already noted, was "a vessel of 120 tons." Another slaver of those days was the *Oak Tree*, "Jansen Eykenboom, from Hoorn, master under God." In a charter-party dated "in the year of the birth of our Lord and Saviour the Lord Jesus Christ, 1659, the 25th of January," under which the *Oak Tree* was to "sail, with the first favourable wind and weather which God may vouchsafe, from the harbor [New York] direct toward the coast of Africa," the size of the ship is given: "In length 120 ft, in width 25½ ft, draft 11 ft, above the waterline 5 to 6 ft, with a poop deck."

36

The average New England slaver was much smaller.
The sloop *Welcome* that cleared from Newport for
Barbadoes had a capacity of 5,000 gallons of molasses. The *Fame*, a noted slaver and privateer of
Newport, had a keel seventy-nine feet long. She was
just about as long on the water-line as the Newport-
built defenders of the America's cup. Her beam was
twenty-six and a half feet, which was about the width
of the widest defender.

The brigantine *Sanderson*, in which Captain David
Lindsay made fame, carried 10,000 gallons of molasses.

A contract made by Caleb Clapp and Stephen
Brown, who were ship-builders at " Warren, in the
County of Bristole, in the colony of Rhode Island,"
in 1747, gives some interesting dimensions of a brigantine they had on the stocks. She was to be "sixty
feet length of keel, straight rabbet, and length of
rake forward to be fourteen feet, three foot and one-
half of which to be put into the keel, so that she will
then be sixty-three feet keel and eleven feet rake forward. Twenty-three feet by the beam, ten feet in the
hold, and three feet ten inches betwixt decks, and
twenty inches waste. Rake abaft to be according to
the usual proportions, to have a sufficient false stern.
Keel to be sided thirteen inches."

A vessel of 500 tons would have, in these days, a
keel no larger than that. The "betwixt decks"
space is worth remembering, because the slaves were
stowed there.

In 1808 the trade was outlawed, while twelve years
later it was declared piracy, and a few war-ships
were sent out to suppress it. Two kinds of vessels

were used thereafter. One kind included slender schooners built for speed ; the other kind included large ships, a few only of which were swift. The large ones were fitted out by men who meant to get rich at a single stroke. The small ones were used by men who found the trade congenial. These last would have been sneak-thieves in a criminal career ashore ; the others, highwaymen.

We have definite figures regarding some of the vessels provided for the sneaking slavers, because some of them were captured and accurate measurements were made. In 1847 the *Felicidade*, of sixty-seven tons; the *Maria*, of thirty tons, and the *Rio Bango*, of ten tons, were captured, all loaded with slaves in a manner to be described further on ; though it may be said here that the *Maria*, a vessel, say, fifty feet long and sixteen wide, had two hundred and thirty-seven on board when taken. Some New York oyster sloops are larger than she was.

The smaller vessels were built, in some cases, in such fashion that the crew could take down the masts and use oars. This gave them every advantage in escaping from the cruisers that must show sails above the horizon when ten miles or more away.

Even the ten-ton schooner was not the limit. Open row-boats no more than twenty-four feet long by seven wide landed as many as thirty-five children in Brazil out of, say, fifty with which the voyage began.

The finest ship of the large class was the *Venus*, a vessel of four hundred and sixty tons, built at Baltimore, at a cost of $30,000. So swift was this vessel that when chased on the coast of Africa her captain actually shortened sail in order to play with the man-o'-war. There was nothing under sail that could equal her in her day. She landed over eight hundred slaves on her first voyage, with a net profit not far from three hundred dollars per head.

A few steamers were known in the trade. The *Providencia* in four voyages landed 4,500 slaves in Brazil. Another one called the *Cacique* is better known. She was originally the *Tigress*, belonging to a Captain Sanford, and was plying between New York and Stonington. Sanford sold her to a Brazilian merchant named Sexias for $11,500. Sexias spent $13,500 in repairs and alterations. " In these transactions Mr. Gardner, an American resident in that city [New York], appears to have acted as agent, and he was looked upon then and afterward, by the Americans belonging to the vessel, as the consignee, and there is reason to believe he engaged in fitting out other steam vessels for the same purpose."

The *Cacique* took on 1,000 slaves at Cabenda and could have made a safe voyage with these, but Sexias waited for the local agents to collect five hundred more and was captured by a British cruiser in consequence.

The old whaler became a favorite slaver type, because her try-pots could cook yams and rice as well as try oil, and her barrels carry either oil or water.

One of the last and undoubtedly the most noted of the whaler-slavers was the bark *Augusta*, of New York. Gilbert H. Cooper testified, after the *Augusta* was seized, that he " purchased portions of the same vessel at the rate of $2,000 for the whole," and that he sold her to Appleton Oaksmith for $4,900, including $1,800 worth of outfittings for the voyage, or $3,100 for the ship alone—"which was $1,000 more than the [other] owners had authorized me to sell her for."

As the eighteenth century passed away the improvements in merchant shipping, so far as improvements were made, were due chiefly to the enterprise of slave-merchants, and at the beginning of the nineteenth century there was nothing afloat of their size that could overhaul the slavers that were turned into privateers during the war of 1812.

In the nineteenth century the slave-trade had relatively much less influence on shipping, but it is certain that the *Venus* from Baltimore was the forerunner of the splendid Yankee clippers whose voyages previous to the Civil War astonished the maritime world. It is certain, too, that the building of small, swift schooners enriched many a Yankee ship-yard owner in the years before our Civil War. If the sole end of government were the promotion of business interests, then it might be said that those officials who winked at the doings of slavers served their country well.

What goods were used in the slave-trade has been recorded in many official documents. Here is the bill of lading of the *Sierra Leone*, a Yankee slaver in the middle of the eighteenth century.

"Shipped by the Grace of GOD in good Order and well conditioned, by William Johnson & Co., owners of the said Schooner, called the *Sierra Leone*, whereof is master under God for this present voyage, David Lindsay, & now riding at Anchor in Harbour of Newport, & by God's grace bound for the Coast of Africa: To say," etc. The usual list of rum, food, and shackles follows, with "sixty musketts, six half barrels Powder" and so on, the bill ending at last with these words: "And so God send the good Schooner to her desired Port in Safety. Amen."

There is no reason to suppose that the invocations to the Deity were a mere vain following of custom. There is the record of "one good old elder, whose ventures on the coast had uniformly turned out well." He "always returned thanks on the Sunday following the arrival of a slaver in the harbor of Newport, that an overruling Providence has been pleased to bring to this land of freedom another cargo of benighted heathen, to enjoy the blessing of a Gospel dispensation." As the author of "Examen de l'Esclavage en Général," a French pro-slavery work, says: "Devotion was at that time the great occupation in Europe ; and it was believed that Christians and sugar might easily be made at the same time."

In 1801, when the prices on the slave-coast were at the highest, the following goods were given for one prime slave. The list is quoted from Gower Williams :

"One piece of chintz, 18 yards long ; one piece of baft, 18 yards long ; one piece of chelloe, 18 yards long ; one piece of bandanoe ; seven handkerchiefs ; one piece of niccannee, 14 yards long ; one piece of cushtae, 14 yards long ; three pieces of romalls ; forty-five handkerchiefs ; one large brass pan ; two muskets ; twenty-five kegs powder ; 100 flints ; two bags of shots ; twenty knives ; four iron pots ; four hats ; four caps ; four cutlasses ; six bunches beads ; fourteen gallons brandy." The total cost of the articles was £25.

The captain of another slave-ship, writing in 1757, gives a list of his cargo as follows :

"Have on bord 140 hhds. Rum for owners, 100 lbs. Provisions, 12 Thousand lbs. bread, six 4-pounders, 4 swevles & 4 cowhorns [a kind of gun], small arms, &c."

In the earliest days rum was the best article for the purchase of slaves. At the end of the eighteenth century, when slaves were obtained chiefly by murderous raids, arms were of first consequence. And then when the slavers established great depots and barracoons on the slave-coast a time came when coin was wanted more than any other commodity.

When Commodore M. C. Perry was in command of the African squadron he sent the following letter to Washington:

UNITED STATES FRIGATE MACEDONIAN,
At Sea, January 28, 1844.

Goods suitable for the African trade, to comprise a cargo for a vessel of two hundred and fifty tons.

40 hogsheads tobacco, long leaf and small head, Virginia. 100 barrels powder, in 10 and 20 pound kegs. American cotton goods, consisting of furniture and apron checks, bleached and unbleached muslins, blue handkerchiefs, calicoes, blue drill, blue bafts or salempores, English dry goods, viz.. blue and white bafts satin stripes, romanes, tomcoffees. 100 barrels beef, pork and mackerel. 100 barrels flour, 25 barrels kiln-dried cornmeal. 2,000 pounds refined sugar, 1,000 pounds brown sugar, 20 kegs butter, 20 kegs lard, 20 boxes sperm candles, 50 boxes soap. 2,000 pounds hams, 1,000 pounds sides and shoulders, 400 pounds beef tongues. 300 pounds cheese, 20 boxes raisins, 50 barrels pilot and navy bread. Half dozen quarter casks of wine, madeira, port and sherry. Tea in two-pound caddies, young hyson and gunpowder, 500 pounds coffee. Crockery, consisting of C. C. wash basins, painted quart and pint mugs and jugs, say 100 dozen of each. Tin pans, assorted sizes, say 50 dozen. Tin buckets with bales, four gallon size, 100 dozen. Wooden buckets, painted, say 25 dozen. Gentlemen's boots and shoes, 100 pairs, assorted, principally large sizes. Ladies' shoes,

kid and prunelle, 100 pairs, assorted. Gentlemen's half hose, ladies' cotton stockings of good quality, 50 dozen each. 100 dozen palm-leaf hats, assorted. Blank books, paper, ink and quills, in equal proportion, say $50 worth. 400 pounds white lead, 30 gallons paint oil, 30 gallons lamp oil. Brass kettles and pans, say 1,000 pounds, two-eighth kettles. About $500 laid out in articles of good quality for ladies ; muslin, lace, insertion, silk gloss, silk stockings, small quantity of black silk, needles, pins, thread in spools and hanks, ribbons for bonnets, a few bonnets &c. 10 boxes good Spanish cigars in quarter boxes. If there be plenty of room, put in 500 feet of boards. 20 kegs of cut nails, assorted sizes, say 4, 6, 7, and 8 penny. 2 dozen silk and 5 dozen cotton umbrellas. A small quantity of ale, porter, and cider, the best quality, say 50 dozen each of ale and porter, and 25 of cider.

Cutlasses and muskets are in demand for trade, but can be furnished much cheaper from England than from the United States. Those brought out are of an inferior quality.

This list has been received from an authentic source, and is now forwarded to the Navy Department, by

M. C. PERRY,
Commanding African Squadron.

NOTE.—Whiskey, or rum, is a profitable article of traffic, but is purposely omitted in this list.

CHAPTER V

ON THE SLAVE-COAST

Physical Features of Land and Sea—Peculiarities of the Aborigines and some Characteristics that were not Peculiar to Them—Gathering Slaves for the Market—A Trade that Degenerated from a System of Fair Barter into the Most Atrocious Forms of Piracy Conceivable—Utter Degradation of White Traders—The Slaughter at Calabar—Prices Paid for Slaves—The Barracoons of Pedro Blanco and Da Souza—When Negroes Voluntarily Sold Themselves.

THE chief source of supply for the devouring slave-market of the West throughout the whole history of the trade, and practically the only source during the years when the trade was legal, was found along the Atlantic coast of Africa, between Cape Verde, at the north, and Benguela, or Cape St. Martha, at the south. The sea here makes a great scoop into the land, as if the Brazilian part of the South American continent had been broken out of the hollow in the African coast. Two great rivers and a host of smaller streams come down to the sea within its limits, and its contour, as a whole, is that of a mighty gulf, but there is neither bay nor inlet throughout its whole extent that forms a good harbor for shipping. And the off-shore islands, too, are few in number and small in extent. The land at the beach is almost everywhere low, even though hills and mountains may be

44

seen, flooded with a dreamy haze, in the distance. The rivers wind about through uncounted channels in low delta lands covered with masses of mangrove and palm trees, and haunted by poisonous and vicious reptiles. The yellowish sand of the sea and the black washings of the uplands mingle to form low, tawny beaches and dunes where the river currents are beaten back by the ever-present and ever-treacherous surf. Goree and Gambia, Sierra Leone and Liberia, the Bight of Benin and the Bight of Biafra, Bonny and Calabar, Anamaboe and Ambriz, the Congo and St. Paul de Loango, are all familiar names to the student of slave-coast literature.

Here as elsewhere in the primitive life of man the strong dominated the weak—there were tribes that were superior, mentally and physically, to their neighbors, and in every tribe there were men who arose above the masses, while among these stalwarts there was a chief who was in every case a real hero to his people. The sons of the chiefs or kings did, indeed, inherit the commanding positions of their fathers, but only when it was shown in them that the blood had not degenerated. In some tribes there was no inheritance of the chief's office.

It was a superstitious as well as a savage people, believing in the existence of invisible supernatural beings of various kinds, but because of the destructive influence of the unexplainable phenomena of nature round about, they regarded nearly all of these spirits as having malevolent minds. From the lightning's stroke to the insidious spread of a tumor, no ill of life occurred that was not the work of a malignant spirit.

In a way not hard to understand, these savages connected the spirits with the evil creatures of the earth —with the poisonous serpents, the fierce robber birds, the ravenous beasts, and with those human individuals in whom cunning and stealth took the place of courage and physical prowess. Even the rocks, when of unusual form, and especially when of terrifying aspect, were regarded as the abiding places of evil spirits, and not infrequently as their visible bodies.

With all they had a crude knowledge of what, in works on political economy, is treated under the head of "exchanges." The savage, of course, had made but slight progress in the practical arts, while the white men understood the results of accumulation as well as of exchange.

In one other matter the savage and the civilized man found themselves on common ground, though that is not to say exactly on a level. They both loved rum. The white man mixed his rum with juice of limes and water and sugar. The savage always took (and takes) his "straight." The white man of those days, too, preferred madeira wine when he could afford it, which he could do after one voyage to Africa. Moreover the white man drank it for his health, or for some other reason of that kind, while the savage took it because he liked it. The relative levels of the two races are herein manifest.

Because the white men were superior in a variety of ways the black men received them with joy, and opened traffic at once.

It was a grewsome traffic that followed—the most grewsome in the history of the world—for the white men came seeking slaves and the blacks had them to sell.

It is a curious subject of inquiry, when we come to consider how the African chiefs happened to have slaves for sale. That slaves were few in number during the earlier years of the trade is certain. That is to say, the great men of every tribe held a few of their neighbors as personal property. They were detained in various ways, but chiefly through taking prisoners in the fights with neighboring tribes, for strange as it may seem now, the presence of slaves in a tribe indicated some degree of mercy in the minds of the slave-owners. Instead of killing everybody, old and young, when attacking an enemy, these slave-owners saved some alive.

One other way was through the tribal laws regarding debts. The civilized people threw the insolvent debtor into prison and held him there, very frequently, until he died—sometimes while he starved to death. The black savages made the debtor work out the debt. It was also noted by the whites that when a negro husband found one of his wives unfaithful he made a slave of her lover.

More remarkable still was another source of slave-owning among the Africans. So jealous were they of their right to worship their gods when, where, and how they pleased, that for a man to desecrate or remove a neighbor's fetish, or even to touch it, was an offence for which the penalty was often slavery.

War, crime, and superstition supplied the great men of the tribes with servants, and these they would sell on occasion. That they might also sell wives and children scarcely need be said, though sons were rarely sold save in time of famine, even in the mild slave-holding days before the white slaver came—days when slaves were, on the whole, treated as members of the slave-holder's family. In connection with these facts we must remember that the Africans, having food and raiment, were therewith content. They did not try to accumulate fortunes, and so had no need for many workmen. Slaves were few in number on this coast before the white man came.

The story of the first American voyage to Africa of which we have a definite record tells us somewhat of methods employed in obtaining slave cargoes. A Boston ship, called the *Rainbowe*, commanded by one Captain Smith, went away to Madeira with salt-fish and staves. Sailing thence with the proceeds of her sale, she "touched on the coast of Guinea" for slaves. She found some London slave-vessels already here, with their captains very much disgruntled because trade was dull. There were very few slaves for sale, that is, and to liven matters a little, the Yankees and the Londoners united, and " on pretence of some quarrel with the natives landed a 'murderer'—the expressive name of a small cannon—attacked a negro village on Sunday, killed many of the inhabitants, and made a few prisoners, two of whom fell to the share of the Boston ship."

That was in 1645—just twenty-six years after the Dutchman landed the slaves in Virginia as recorded by John Rolfe, the first American squaw-man. False pretence, outrage, and the slaughter of innocents characterized the first-recorded gathering of slaves in which an American had part. They "killed many of

AFTER A RAID.

See page 56.

the inhabitants," and got two slaves for their share of the plunder.

That Captain Smith's act was not according to the ordinary usages of the trade may be inferred from what happened when he returned to Boston. A quarrel with the ship's owners over the proceeds of the voyage resulted in a lawsuit. The story of the voyage was told in court, and although it was not a criminal trial, one of the magistrates "charged the master with a threefold offence—murder, man-stealing, and Sabbath-breaking." The captain escaped punishment on these charges, on the ground that the court had no jurisdiction over crimes committed in Africa, a decision that was typical of what was to come. But the two slaves were returned home.

On the other hand, when we consider the usual course of trade, we may say that, viewed fairly and by the light of the age, the gathering of slaves on the coast of Africa, previous to 1750, was conducted with as great a regard for honesty as was any other trade with uncivilized people.

The voyage to the coast in the Newport slaver days lasted anywhere from six to ten weeks, according to the ship and the luck in winds. On reaching Bonny, or Anamaboe, or Old Calabar, then favorite ports, the captain made ready for a grand entertainment in honor of the native chiefs and headmen. To put it bluntly, the chiefs were invited on board to get drunk, and they accepted the invitation with an eager thirst.

In addition to this free debauch the chiefs received sundry presents. According to Alexander Falconbridge, a surgeon in the trade in the latter half of the

4

eighteenth century, the presents "generally consist of pieces of cloth, cotton, chintz, silk handkerchiefs, and other India goods, and sometimes brandy, wine, or beer."

Having propitiated the chiefs, the captain was free to begin trade. Some inkling of how this was conducted is told in the letter of Captain George Scott in the chapter "When Voyages Went Awry."

It was disheartening and even exasperating to the slavers, and the more enterprising made ways of livening the trade. They looked for a chief who held a grudge against a native tribe, and incited and aided him to take revenge. They suggested to chiefs that certain stout, well-built citizens of the tribe were ambitious of becoming rulers and that an effectual stop to such ambition was to sell the offenders. They made friends with the fetish or medicine men—always the adroit and underhand rascals of the tribe—in order to have charges of witchcraft preferred against likely young men and women. They persuaded the medicine men to have youths and children entrapped without any charge of any kind. They told men having many wives that this or that young man was the lover of one or another wife. So the great man was led to lie in wait and capture the lover and sell him. It was a short step from this to another practice whereby attractive wives were sent to entrap unwary amorous swains. Incredible as it must seem, the civilized captains from Christian lands introduced what is known to professional thieves as the badger game, and they made money out of it, and the ship merchants and stockholders in the ships knew that it was done and willingly shared the profits.

But a worse state of affairs was to come. That there was a steady growth in the number of ships in the trade has already been noted. The cause of the rapid increase in the number and capacity of the slavers during the middle years of the eighteenth century is not far to seek. The planters of the West Indies had found it more profitable to work slaves to death, while yet in the prime of life, than to support them in an idle old age. The loss of hands could be readily replaced by importations from Africa, and there was nothing in the civilization of that age to make the planters consider any other question in the matter than that of making profits.

The prices of slaves rose steadily under this increasing demand. Captain Lindsay, in the voyage that was "anoof to make a man creasey," sold his prime slaves for £35 each. Twenty-five years later the price received averaged £70, and the Liverpool ship *Enterprise*, belonging to T. Leyland & Co., in a voyage made about the first of the present century, cleared £24,430 8s. 11d. on a cargo of three hundred and ninety-two slaves, or more than £62 per head, old and young all counted in.

The result was an activity, well called "feverish," in the market on the African coast. The price of a slave there, according to a Newport record dated 1762, was one hundred and ten gallons of rum. An old commercial history of Liverpool records that in 1786 the average cost of delivering a slave in the West Indies was £27 5s. 10d., of which perhaps £22 was the price paid for the slave. With the first jumps in the price came a change in the methods of obtaining cargoes. The dribbling supply that had worried Captain

Lindsay, who was satisfied with a cargo of but fifty-six, was wholly inadequate to the growing demand.

The first change in the trade was relatively a mild one. Slavers had never been very scrupulous about the title which a seller claimed when a slave was offered, but there are cases on record where slavers refused to buy when it was learned that men offered as slaves were really free and had been kidnapped. When the demand became eager, after 1750, the captains let it be known that every soul offered, if physically sound, would be taken and no questions asked. Slaves, too, had been purchased almost exclusively of chiefs and headmen, and it had been a daylight trade. Now anybody might bring a slave at any time of the night and get a good price for him.

Straightway the people of the coast who, in the ordinary course of their lives would never have owned a slave, began bringing slaves to the ships. Two or three would paddle off in a canoe at night, bringing one that was bound and gagged, and the purchase of those who were manifestly kidnapped became the regular custom of the trade. Alexander Falconbridge, the slaver surgeon already quoted, said that in his time (during the latter part of the century) the majority of the slaves with whom he talked had been kidnapped. He gave many instances of which he had personal knowledge, by way of illustration. A woman was invited by a neighbor to come in for a visit one evening. As soon as she entered the hut two men in waiting bound her and carried her on board ship. A father and his son, while planting yams, were seized by men who came from the brush. A man from the interior having brought some product to the beach for sale was asked to visit the ship lying off shore and get a free drink of rum. He went, but when there found that his guide had sold him, and stay he must.

James Town, a ship carpenter, in the Parliamentary inquiry, testified that he saw a dealer sell a slave on board a ship, in the Gallinas, but when the dealer paddled to the beach with his goods, four men came from the brush, seized him, robbed him of his goods and then carried him, in his own canoe, to the slave-ship, where they sold him to the captain, who had seen the whole doings.

While the British slaver *Briton* was lying in the Benin River a native chief known as Captain Lemma came on board to get the usual presents. A few minutes later a canoe with three negroes was seen crossing the river, and the chief sent his followers to bring it to the ship. The three proved to be members of another tribe than the chief's, and they were at once offered for sale. Two were purchased, but the third, an elderly man, was refused as unsalable. At that the old man was taken over the rail and there his head was cut off.

Off Piccaninni Sestus, on the windward coast, in 1769, Mr. William Dove saw a noted native slaver named Ben Johnson bring off a girl he had stolen. Just as Johnson was leaving the ship on one side two very excited men came to the other to inquire about the girl. On learning her fate they went in chase of Johnson, captured him, and, bringing him to the ship, offered him for sale.

"You won't buy me, whom you know to be a great

trading man, will you, captain?" said Johnson, in
remonstrance.

"If they will sell you I will buy you, be you what
you may," replied the captain, and the kidnapping Ben
Johnson became a slave himself. This story is especially interesting because of the picture it gives of the
workings of the captain's mind. He would not kidnap
a negro himself, but he would buy of anyone under
any circumstances.

A man named Marsh, who was in charge of a shore
station established for buying slaves at Cape Coast
Castle, in those days, is on record as saying: "I do
not mind how they get them, for I buy them fairly."
It is a queer exhibition of conscientious scruples,
though one, perhaps, not now wholly unknown.

But the slavers rapidly outgrew such squeamishness.
They outgrew it simply because the increased numbers
obtained by such methods were still inadequate for
the demand. Moreover with the increase in the number in an average cargo came a special need for haste
in procuring them. Captain Lindsay might keep forty
negroes "in helth and fatt" under the deck of the
Sanderson while gathering fifteen or twenty more by
the old slow process, but when Captain Billy Boates,
of Liverpool, a noted slaver, who was "born a beggar
to die a lord," had two hundred and fifty on board
the ship *Knight*, in which he won fame, he could not
wait long for the remaining hundred because those
already on board would die.

The trade in its origin had been an exchange of a
fair measure of goods for individuals legally held
as slaves. It arrived at a stage in which a majority
of every cargo purchased consisted of freemen kid-

napped as individuals. The next step down involved a resort to piracy—to deliberate attacks on natives who refused to trade. It will be remembered that the Massachusetts slaver had been a pirate in this fashion as early as 1645. Such acts were too common throughout the traffic, but what is to be emphasized here is that piratical acts naturally increased in number as the demand for slaves increased.

Following bloody quarrels with the coast tribes came the practice of inciting the coast tribes to make piratical raids on the interior.

It is likely that the practice of inciting these raids began as early as 1757—perhaps earlier, in a desultory way. At any rate, in a letter already quoted "six four-pounders, four swevles, and four cow-horns" were among the goods carried out for trade. But it is certain that raiding was not then the usual course of trade.

Mr. John Bowman, who was employed at the slave coast just previous to 1776, testified before the Committee of Parliament that he had had charge of an agency established on the Scassus River for supplying the warlike natives with arms for raids, and that he accompanied the raiders on one expedition. Coming to the agency the chief obtained a supply of guns and ammunition. Then the trumpets were sounded, a band of men was collected, the arms were distributed, and the start was made immediately. Late in the afternoon the band camped near a branch of the Scassus and waited until midnight. Then, leaving Bowman, whose heart had failed him, they crept away through the forest. A half hour later shouts and screams were heard and the forest was lighted up by the flames of burning huts. Later still the band returned, bringing thirty men, women, and children. A small village had been attacked when all its people were asleep. Some were killed and some escaped to the brush, the thirty captives being taken alive and unhurt. These were bound securely, and when day came they were carried down to the agency.

This is one of the mildest stories of a raid known to the history of the trade.

Captain Canot, in describing the work of a raiding party, says:

"In my wanderings in Africa I have often seen the tiger pounce upon its prey, and with instinctive thirst satiate its appetite for blood and abandon the drained corpse; but these African negresses [who were of the raiding party] were neither as decent nor as merciful as the beast of the wilderness. Their malignant pleasure seemed to consist in the invention of tortures that would agonize but not slay. A slow, lingering, tormenting mutilation was practised on the living . . . and in every instance the brutality of the women exceeded that of the men. I cannot picture their hellish joy . . . while the queen of the harpies crept amid the butchery gathering the brains from each severed skull as a *bonne bouche* for the approaching feast."

As for the defeated negroes who were not killed, they were carried down to the sea and sold. And as time passed the passion for blood grew on the raiders until it was greater than their greed. They tortured to death many whom they might have sold. Before the end of the eighteenth century these raids, called wars by those who owned the slave-ships, were the chief source of supply for the coast market, and after the trade was declared illegal they were, practically, the only source of supply ; and the people of the United States knew that it was so.

There were many little tribes and settlements on the rivers in the old days wherein the natives were chiefly devoted to agriculture, and these were the prey of the coast pirates until the rivers were swept clean of all peace-loving inhabitants, and the whole population surviving was turned into ravaging pirate bands.

Said an eloquent coast chief when the English began to negotiate with him for the abolition of the slave traffic:

"I and my army are ready, at all times, to fight the enemies of England, and do anything the English may ask of me, except to give up the slave-trade. No other trade is known to my people. It is the source of their glory and wealth. Their songs celebrate their victories, and the mother lulls the child to sleep with notes of triumph over an enemy reduced to slavery."

Still another view of the effect of the growing demand for slaves is to be given. "Treat men as pawns and nine-pins and you shall suffer as well as they." It is chiefly because of the effect of the trade on those engaged in it, directly or indirectly, that their history is of present interest.

From furnishing arms to raiders and otherwise inciting them to the work, the white slavers at an early day descended far enough to take part in the bloody deeds. Even Anglo-Saxon slavers—members of the only race that in these days does really understand the meaning of the words justice and liberty—were found ready to pose as peacemakers for the purpose of betraying one band of negroes into the hands of another, and of themselves beginning the bloody slaughter that followed.

The Calabar (or Kalaba) River empties into the Bight of Biafra—right at the angle formed by the coast lines of the huge gulf already mentioned. It is a stream about three miles wide, with from three to five fathoms of water. The banks are low and covered with mangrove brush and palm-trees. Numerous lagoons are found on both sides of the stream, and the apparent banks are but a succession of islands.

On one of these islands was a settlement known as Old Calabar, or the Old Town. On another was a settlement called New Town. The people of the two settlements were of one blood, but they hated each other intensely because of the rivalry growing out of the slave trade. Yet so nearly balanced were they in forces that only by kidnapping and an occasional murder of an individual or two could one inflict injury on the other. However, as time went on the New Town people became somewhat the stronger through favor of the slave captains, and then came the crowning infamy of the trade in that age.

It was in the year 1767. The ships *Indian Queen*, *Duke of York*, *Nancy*, and *Concord*, of Bristol ; the *Edgar*, of Liverpool and the *Canterbury*, of London, were lying in the river between the two towns. Trade was dull, and the captains of these ships got together to devise a plan to liven it by taking advantage of the jealousy between the two towns, and the somewhat superior force of New Town. After brief consultation it was agreed that they should, on the pretence of making peace between the two towns, invite the Old Town people to come unarmed to the ships for a palaver. Accordingly messages were sent to the chief, Ephraim Robin John, his brother, Amboe, and some other headmen, requesting all the men of the town to come to the ships on a certain day, and promising unlimited free rum to mellow the hearts of the obdurate before the peace terms were arranged. The captains, of course, pledged their honor to protect the Old Town people from all danger during the palaver, and a safe return ashore.

Knowing their inferiority in fighting force, the Old Calabar people very gladly accepted the offer of these ship-captains to arrange for peace, and the appointed day came on with much jubilation in Old Calabar. For some reason not given Chief Ephraim did not go off to the banquet, but he sent one of his wives as a present to the Chief of New Town ; and three of his brothers, of whom Amboe was the oldest, went in one canoe along with twenty-seven other men, while nine other canoes, none of which was smaller than this, followed.

The first ship visited was the *Indian Queen*, where a seemingly hearty welcome was extended. From the *Indian Queen* the leading canoe was sent to the *Edgar* and thence to the *Duke of York*, an abundance of rum being supplied at each ship. Some of the canoes followed the leader, and others distributed themselves among the other ships, where the greater number of their crews went on board and were received with lavish presents of rum.

The effect of the liquor was soon apparent in the

sleepy actions of the drinkers, and the moment for the final stroke of the conspiracy was at hand. While Amboe Robin John and his two brothers were sitting in the cabin of the *Duke of York* her officers and crew suddenly dropped the rum-cups, and, taking up muskets, cutlasses, and boarding-pikes, that had been placed ready for the occasion, they attacked the unsuspecting and unarmed negroes.

A wild dash for life was made. The three brothers strove to get out of the cabin-windows, but were hauled in and ironed. On deck the negroes who strove to resist were cut down, and those who fled for the rail were tripped or slashed or stabbed or shot, as the case might be. Even the canoes alongside were fired on and sunk with all who happened to be in them, when some were drowned, some were dragged on board, and a few went swimming for the shore.

The noise of the conflict on the *Duke of York* was a signal to the other ships, on most of which the natives were attacked in like manner. And then came the inhabitants of the New Town; for the slaver captains had arranged that they should hide in the mangroves along shore until the attack was made, when they were to come out with canoes and pick up the Old Town people who might be swimming for the shore. And these, being mad with their thirst for blood, killed more than they took out of the water for slaves. In all more than three hundred of the Old Town people were killed or enslaved in the course of this raid planned by the white men.

But the end of the story is not yet told. Having killed or captured the last man in the water, the New Town people paddled to the ships to receive their re-

ward for their share in the onslaught. This reward
was collected, of course, in the shape of a liberal price
for each captured Old Town man, with free drinks
added, although of the drinks they were naturally a
little shy under the circumstances. But at the side of
the *Duke of York*, one other reward was wanted—the
head of their chief enemy among the captured Old
Town people—the head of Amboe Robin John. But
knowing that the captain of the *Duke of York* cared
nothing for their thirst for blood—knowing that he had
joined in the raid solely for the profit there was in it—
the chief of New Town, who was known as Willy
Honesty, said :

"Captain, if you will give me that man, to cut his
head off, I will give you the best man in my canoe,
and you shall be slaved first ship."

At that Amboe, who could speak English, bowed his
head and, putting his hands together in the attitude of
prayer, begged the captain of the ship to retain him
on board. But the captain forced him, his guest
under a solemn promise of protection, over the rail,
where his head was struck off, and his body thrown to
the sharks.

As a result of their treachery and murder, the slaver
captains received from twenty-five to thirty slaves
each, of whom a third, perhaps, were captured in
the water, and had to be purchased of the New Town
people.

The two brothers of Amboe Robin John were sold in
the West Indies, but managed to escape to Virginia,
and thence to Bristol, "where the captain who had
brought them, fearing he had done wrong, meditated
carrying them back." But before he could sail with

them, a shipper in the oil, ivory, and gold-dust trade, who had heard the story of the massacre, took them before a court on a writ of *habeas corpus*, when they were declared free and were sent home to Old Calabar. Through this means Clarkson, the famous abolitionist, got the authenticated story, and used it with tremendous effect in his crusade against the trade. It was not in the Anglo-Saxon heart to approve such doings, even in the eighteenth century.

Time had been when the long and dangerous voyage had made vikings of those engaged in it, but as the profits grew and swelled before the eyes of the slavers all other views were fogged from sight, and from brave men, really striving to do right, they were, within half a century, degraded to a level beyond which there was no depth conceivable. And degradation is the inevitable fate of everyone who deliberately ignores justice in his treatment of inferiors. Get rich he may, but be degraded hell-low he shall be.

How the degradation of the slaver's deck was contagious; how it spread to the owners of the ships; how these owners, while posing as Christians, became, through inciting such acts, worse than the captains who participated actively in the infamies; how communities and nations were thus made rotten, until at last the greatest slave nation of them all regained health by the most frightful of modern wars, can only be suggested here.

After the end of the eighteenth century the only notable change in the methods of gathering slaves for market was in the establishing of barracoons—that is, what a cowboy might call corrals—in which to herd the slaves awaiting shipment. The trade having been outlawed, cruisers were stationed on the African coast to stop the work of the slavers. The slave-ships then had need of such quick despatch as had never been dreamed of before. They came to the coast, usually, disguised as honest traders, and watching for a day when the coast was clear they got their slaves quickly on board and sailed away. To enable a ship to load quickly, depots were established at convenient points, where pens were built by setting tree-trunks into the ground to make a high fence. In these the slaves were held by the hundred—sometimes more than a thousand were imprisoned in one pen—to await the arrival of a ship.

Captain Philip Drake, an English slaver, whose diary was printed in New York about forty years ago under the title of "Revelations of a Slave-Smuggler," describes incidentally two of the most noted of these slave stations—that of Don Pedro Blanco, on the Gallinas River, and that of Da Souza, at Whydah. "Gallinas," he says, "was a depot and market for slaves brought from all streams that penetrated the Guinea Coast, as well as territory further south. The river was full of small islands ; and on several of these, near the sea, as well as on the banks, were located factories, barracoons, dwelling-houses, and storehouses. The success of Blanco had attracted a dozen other traders, and the Don was a prince among them. In African fashion he supported a harem, and quite a retinue of house servants, guards, etc., besides clerks and overseers of his barracoons."

Captain Canot describes Blanco's headquarters in greater detail. He says :

" About a mile from the river's mouth we found a

group of islets on each of which was erected the factory of some particular slave-merchant belonging to the grand confederacy. Blanco's establishments were on several of these marshy flats. On one, near the mouth, he had his place of business or trade with foreign vessels, presided over by his principal clerk, an astute and clever gentleman. On another island, more remote, was his residence, where a sister, for a while, shared with Don Pedro his solitary home.* Here this man of education and refined address surrounded himself with every luxury that could be purchased in Europe or the Indies, and dwelt in a sort of Oriental but semi-barbarous splendor. Further inland was another islet, devoted to his seraglio, within whose recesses each of his favorites inhabited her separate establishment after the fashion of the natives.

"The barracoons were made of rough poles of the hardest trees, four or six inches in diameter, driven five feet in the ground and clamped together by double rows of iron bars. Their roofs were constructed of similar wood, strongly secured, and overlaid with a thick thatch of long and wiry grass, rendering the interior both dry and cool. Watch-houses, built near the entrance, were tenanted by sentinels, with loaded muskets. Each barracoon was tended by two or four Spaniards or Portuguese, but I have rarely met a more wretched class of human beings. Such were the surroundings of Don Pedro in 1836. Three years later he left the coast forever with a fortune of nearly a million."

* There are records of more than one woman being engaged in the slave-trade on her own account.

A WILD DASH FOR LIFE WAS MADE.

See page 60.

Captain Drake, under date of January 5, 1840, writes of another coast prince as follows :

" Da Souza, or Cha-Chu, as everybody calls him, is apparently a reckless voluptuary, but the shrewdest slave-trader on the African coast. Whydah was built by his enterprise, and he lives the life of a prince. His mansion here is like a palace, and he has a harem filled with women from all parts of the world. He keeps up a continual round of dissipation, gambling, feasting, and indulging in every sensual pleasure with his women and visitors. . . . His house is the very abode of luxury. He must squander thousands. But what is money to a man who has a slave-mine in Dahomey, bringing hoards of wealth yearly by a hundred vessels. Da Souza enjoys almost a monopoly of the coast trade. Blanco has been his only rival of late years. . . . This morning Cha-Chu met me and proposed to supply me with a wife. ' You shall have French, Spanish, Greek, Circassian, English, Dutch, Italian, Asiatic, African or American,' he said laughing."

The origin of the demand for silks and other fancy goods of which Commodore Perry made mention is thus apparent.

The kidnapping and the raiding were increased, although the market price of slaves fell as low as from $12 to $20 a head. The demand continued because the hardships of the slave-life killed off the slaves more rapidly than slave children were born. This was true even in certain parts of the United States. Virginia and some other States were breeding places, but by a statement printed in *De Bow's Review* for November, 1858, it appears that the slave population

of Louisiana in 1850 was 244,985. The report of the
State Auditors to the Legislature of 1858 puts it at
"264,985, an increase of 20,167, or twelve and one-half
per cent., in seven years." The slaves had increased
at the rate of less than 3,000 a year in spite of the importation of thousands from the slave-breeding States
and the smuggling of native Africans!

The raids were extended hundreds of miles inland,
according to Canot. In the atrocities of the raids
there could be no change for the worse, because
there was no form of torture or degradation below that already existing. There was a greater volume of suffering; there could be no worse degree
of it.

The history of the slave-trade is in one respect
unique. In all other forms of industry there was a
steady amelioration of the people engaged in them as
civilization grew brighter. On the sea for instance,
the cat was abolished as a lawful instrument of dis-
cipline and impressment was abandoned. Even in
the killing of cattle humane methods came to be
adopted. But the handling of slaves, from the beginning of the trade to its end, was like a portrayal of
the myth of the bottomless pit.

And yet, black as was the panorama of the trade as
described in history, there was one dash of warm
color in it to relieve the aching heart of the spectator.
Says Charles W. Thomas, U. S. N., chaplain to the
African squadron in 1855, in a work relating to coast
usages:

"In time of famine men who have no slaves to dispose of, or not enough to meet the demand, pawn
themselves . . . for food. . . . A degree of ad-

mirable self-immolation is sometimes shown in such cases of family distress by a member coming forward and offering himself to the highest bidder, willing to go anywhere or to be anything so that he may relieve his father and mother or other dear relatives from distress."

CHAPTER VI

THE MIDDLE PASSAGE

Stowing Slaves for the Voyage from Africa to a Market—The Galleries—Compelled to Lie " Spoon-fashion" to Save Deck Space—A Plan by which the 'Tween Decks Space was Packed Full—Effects of the Ship's Rolling on the Manacled Cargo—Living Slaves Jettisoned to Make a Claim on the Underwriters—Horrors of " The Blood-Stained *Gloria* "— Blinded Crews of the *Rodeur* and the *Leon*—Suicide Among the Tortured Slaves—Pitiful Tale of a Weanling's Death—Punishing Mutiny on the American Slaver *Kentucky*—Slave Ships Named for Two of Our Presidents.

THE term Middle Passage arose from the fact that each slaving voyage was made up of three passages— the passage from the home port to the slave coast, the passage from the slave coast to the market, and the passage from that market back to the home port— say, Newport or Liverpool. It was during the middle of the three passages that the slaves were on board. This passage was invariably made, of course, from the east to the west, and the route lay, for the greater part of its length, in the torrid zone, even when the slaves were destined for the United States.

Most of the ships built for the trade in the eighteenth century had two decks. The space between the keel and the lower deck was called the lower hold, while the space between the two decks was sometimes

called the upper hold, but was generally designated
"'tween decks." The 'tween-deck space was reserved
for the slaves. The new slaver built at "Warren in the
county of Bristole, in the colony of Rhode Island,"
was to be "ten feet in the hold, with three feet ten
inches betwixt decks." That is to say, the space between the decks where the slaves were to be kept
during the time the cargo was accumulating (three to
ten months) and while crossing the Atlantic (six to ten
weeks) was a room as long and as wide as the ship, but
only three feet ten inches high—the space of an average Newport slaver in the days when the traffic was
lawful and respected.

The men were ironed together, two and two by the
ankles, but women and children were left unironed.
They were then taken to the slave-deck, the males forward of a bulkhead built abaft the main hatch, and
the women aft. There all were compelled to lie down
with their backs on the deck and feet outboard. In
this position the irons on the men were usually secured
to chains or iron rods that were rove through staples
in the deck, or the ceiling of the ship. The entire deck
was covered with them lying so. They were squeezed
so tightly together, in fact, that the average space
allowed to each one was but sixteen inches wide by five
and a half feet long.

In the Liverpool ships in the latter part of the eighteenth century—ships that carried from three hundred to five hundred slaves at a load—the average
height between the two decks was five feet two inches.
This statement of the average distance between decks
was proven by measuring many ships. But that is not
to say that the slaves were more comfortable on the

ships having greater space between decks. On the contrary, they were less so. Economy of space was studied with a sharp eye. It would never do to allow all that space between decks to remain unoccupied. So a shelf or gallery, usually six feet wide, was suspended midway between the two decks, and on this another layer of slaves was placed Of course the deck under the shelf or gallery was covered with slaves packed as closely together as possible. This shelf was made of unplaned lumber, and there was no effort to make tight the joints between the boards.

The smaller ships—the sloops and schooners that had no 'tween-decks—were arranged for stowing the slaves by building a temporary deck beneath the upper one. Having stowed the barrels of food and water in the hold so as to occupy as little space as possible, a row of stanchions, fore and aft on the keelson, and rising just above the barrels, was erected. These were connected by a ridge-pole, and from this ridge-pole rafters were extended to the sides of the ship. On the rafters common unplaned boards were laid. Thus a deck was laid that could be easily removed on occasion.

The space between this deck and the upper one was rarely, if ever, more than three feet high, and cases are on record where it was considerably less than two feet—in this century even as little as eighteen inches.

Most of the vessels used after the trade was outlawed were of the small, single-decked class. Because the trade was unlawful these slavers had to be prepared to pass as palm-oil buyers when they were overhauled by a cruiser, and they could not do that if they had a slave-deck laid. Accordingly the slave-

deck was not laid until the slaves were on the beach
ready to embark. Being then in great haste the slaver
did not usually go to the trouble of erecting stanchions
and building his deck substantially. He merely laid
his rafters or timbers on the barrels, as best he might ;
spread the boards over them, with a nail driven in here
and there, perhaps, but sometimes with never a nail to
hold them in place, and then the slaves were brought
on board and jammed into the thin space with less
regard for their comfort than is shown now for hogs
shipped in a two-deck stock-car.

In fact, when the cruisers became at last somewhat
vigilant, cargoes were shipped in vessels that had no
slave-deck ; the slaves were piled on the barrels of food
and water until the barrels were blanketed out of
sight.

But the limit of devilish ingenuity in stowing slaves
was not reached until the trade was outlawed. To increase the number of slaves on the deck they were then
compelled to lie on their sides, breast to back, "spoon
fashion," to use the term then common. Where the
'tween-deck space was two feet high or more the slaves
were stowed sitting up in rows, one crowded into the
lap of another, and with legs on legs, like riders on a
crowded toboggan. In storms the sailors had to put
on the hatches, and seal tight the openings into the
infernal cesspool. It was asserted by the naval officers
who were stationed on the coast to stop the traffic that
in certain states of the weather they could detect the
odor of a slaver further away than they could see her
on a clear night. The odor was often unmistakable
at a distance of five miles down wind.

It was possible for a humane ship-master, such as

Captain Hugh Crow, the one-eyed slaver of Liverpool, by alleviating the sufferings of the slaves by means of good food, daily washings, and some effort to make them cheerful, such as playing musical instruments, etc., to keep the death rate down to one or two per centum. Captain John Newton, who became a famous preacher, says regarding his own experience:

"I had the pleasure to return thanks in the churches for an African voyage performed without any accident or the loss of a man; and it was much noticed and acknowledged in the town. I question if it is not the only instance of the kind. . . . It [the slave-trade] is, indeed, accounted a genteel employment, and is usually very profitable."

Other captains did carry a cargo each without the loss of a man, but such passages were rare. The ordinary slaver captain at the end of the eighteenth century was not so careful, while many a slaver was simply without any sympathy for the unfortunates.

The story of the *Zong*, Captain Luke Collingwood, illustrates this statement. The *Zong* sailed from the island of St. Thomas, off the coast of Africa, on September 6, 1781, bound for Jamaica, with four hundred and forty slaves. The water on board was insufficient in quantity, and the slaves began to die for want of it. On arriving off Jamaica, Collingwood made the mistake of supposing he was off Hayti, and the death-rate was now so great that he began to think the voyage would be unprofitable. On casting about for some way of saving the owners from the impending loss of profits, Captain Collingwood remembered that the underwriters were always obliged to pay for all cargo jettisoned—thrown overboard—either to lighten the

EVERY SOUL ON BOARD WAS BLIND.

See page 76.

ship or to provide in any way for the safety of the cargo retained on board. In short, if the slaves died of disease or from lack of water while on board the ship, the loss would fall on the ship; but if he threw overboard some of them so that he would have enough food and water to abundantly nourish those remaining, he could collect the price of those thrown into the sea from the underwriters.

Accordingly, one hundred and thirty-two of the most wretched slaves were brought on deck. Of these one hundred and twenty-two were thrown to the sharks that swarmed about the ship; but ten, seeing that they were to be thrown over, and that most of the sufferers were writhing in abject terror—these ten struggled to their feet, and, in spite of cramps and weakness, staggered to the rail and plunged over, that they might show the others how to die.

The underwriters refused to pay, however; the case went to court, and the jury decided in favor of the ship. Solicitor-General J. Lee refused to carry the case to a higher court. He said the master had "an unquestionable right" to throw the slaves into the sea.

"This is a case of goods and chattels," said he. "It is really so; it is a case of throwing over goods; for to this purpose, and the purpose of insurance, they are goods and property."

The insurers appealed the case, and the court above, Lord Mansfield, presiding, in spite of the plain mandate of statute—disregarding the obvious meaning of the laws, with the making of which he had nothing to do—*yielded to his sense of humanity*, decided according to "the higher law," and said, "It is a very shocking case." He granted a new trial, at which the insurers escaped paying for the loss. So the laws, being unjust, were violated — disregarded even — by the courts before they were repealed. Such sacrifice of a part of a cargo of slaves to save the others was common enough in the history of the trade.

For a picture of a slaver of the lower class take that given by Drake in his " Revelations of a Slave-Smuggler." He says :

We had left the Verds, and were making southerly in ballast, when we overhauled a Portuguese schooner, and ran alongside. She had a full cargo of slaves, with a large quantity of gold-dust, and our captain, Ruiz, proposed to attack her. The crew were ready, and, inspired by rum, soon mastered the schooner's hands ; our captain blowing out the brains of a passenger, who owned the gold. Some of the Portuguese leaped overboard, with spars ; but Ruiz had a boat manned, and knocked the survivors on the head with axes. The gold-dust and negroes were then quickly transferred to the slaver, the schooner was scuttled, and we kept on our way to the land with 190 slaves. . . . We then ran for Accra, and landed at Papoe, a town belonging to a Dahoman chief, where we found 600 negroes, waiting for a Spanish slaver, soon expected. Ruiz bought 400 of these, paying in the Portuguese gold-dust, and hauled our course for the Atlantic voyage.

But this was to be my last trip in the blood-stained *Gloria*. Hardly were we out a fortnight before it was discovered that our roystering crew had neglected to change the sea-water which had served as our ballast, in the lower casks, and which ought to have been replaced with fresh water in Africa. We were drawing from the last casks before this discovery was made ; and the horror of our situation sobered Captain Ruiz. He gave orders to hoist the precious remnant abaft the main grating, and made me calculate how long it would sustain the crew and cargo. I found that half a gill a day would hold out to the Spanish main ; and it was decided that, in order to save our cargo, we should allow the slaves a half gill, and the crew a gill, each day. Then began a torture worse than death to the blacks. Pent in their close dungeons, to the number of nearly five hundred, they suffered continual torment. Our crew and drivers were unwilling to allow even the half gill per diem, and quarrelled fiercely over their own stinted rations. Our cargo had been stowed on the platforms closer than I ever saw slaves stowed before or since. Instead of lowering buckets of water to them, as was customary, it became necessary to pour the water into half-pint measures. Those furthest from the gratings never got a drop. . . . Death followed so fast that in a short time at least a hundred men and women were shackled to dead partners. Our captain and crew, as well as myself, drank hard. . . . The dead were not thrown overboard. At last Captain Ruiz ordered the hatches down, and swore he would make the run on our regular water rations, and take the chances of his stock.

That night we caroused, and satisfied our thirst, whilst the negroes suffocated below. Next morning came a storm, which drove us on our course a hundred knots. Two days afterward, Ruiz and four of the men were taken suddenly ill with a disease that baffled my medical knowledge. Their tongues swelled, and grew black ; their flesh turned yellow, and in six hours they were dead. The first mate went next, and then three others of the crew, and a black driver, whose body became leprous with yellow spots. I began to notice a strange, fetid smell pervading the vessel, and a low, heavy fog on deck, almost like steam. Then the horrid truth became apparent. Our rotting negroes under hatches had generated the plague, and it was a malaria or death-mist that I saw rising. At this time all our men but three and myself had been attacked ; and we abandoned the *Gloria*, in her long boat, taking the remnant of water, a sack of biscuit, and a rum beaker, with what gold-dust and other valuables we could hastily gather up. We left nine of our late comrades dead and five dying on the *Gloria's* deck. After running for two days we struck a current, and in three more were drifted to the island of Tortola.

People familiar with Whittier's poems will recall "The Slave Ships," founded on the experience of the French slaver *Rodeur*. In 1819 while she was on her way to Guadeloupe with but one hundred and sixty-two slaves on board, a disease of the eyes appeared in the hold and spread rapidly. To save the unaffected and to ground a claim on the underwriters, the captain threw thirty-six of the negroes alive into the sea. The disease continued its ravages, however, and soon attacked the crew with such malignancy that in a short time all but one of them became blind.

In this terrorful condition a sail was seen, and the one man who had the use of his eyes steered the *Rodeur* toward her. In a short time she was seen to be drifting derelict with all sail set, though men were wandering about her deck. The man on the *Rodeur* hailed her, and then her crew swarmed to her rail and begged for help, saying that she was the Spanish slaver *Leon*, and that every soul on board was blind through the ophthalmia generated among the slaves.

The *Rodeur* reached port steered by the one man, but he went blind on reaching shore. The *Leon* was never seen again.

To the stories of the ills of the Middle Passage so far given must be added those which relate to the mental sufferings of the slaves and those that grew out of the deliberate cruelty of the crews. Indeed it is not to much to say that the saddest result of the slave trade now visible is the mental attitude of the white race of America toward the colored.

"The ships," said Dr. Alexander Falconbridge, of the slaver *Tartar*, "were fitted up with a view of preventing slaves jumping overboard," but an opening was left in the netting set above the rail in order that refuse might be dumped overboard, and through this many a negro leaped to his death. Others managed to secrete rope-yarn or strong twine, by which a noose was made and secured to a cleat overhead, and so the slave strangled himself to death. One tore his throat open with his finger-nails. Many others, to kill themselves, refused to eat. They were flogged to compel them to eat, but this failed so often that it was the custom for all slavers to carry a tube-like instrument used by surgeons to force food into the mouths of patients suffering from lockjaw. This was driven into the mouths of obstinate negroes, smashing lips and teeth, until food could be forced down the throat. Instances were described where the lips were burned with coals and hot irons to compel the negroes to open their mouths and swallow the food.

How men and women were flogged to death; how they died smiling under the blows, saying, "Soon we shall be free"; how they leaped overboard and exultingly bade farewell to friends who rejoiced in their escape—all that has been told over and again by the slaver captains themselves.

One of the most pitiful stories known to these annals is told in connection with the slaver habit of compelling his slaves to eat. There was a child, less than a year old, that could not eat the boiled rice prepared for it, and the captain decided that it was stubborn, rather than sick. Getting angry as the little one repeatedly turned its head from the food, he grabbed it from its mother's arms. He tied a twelve-pound stick of wood to its neck as a punishment, and thereafter flogged it with the cat at each meal-time until the fourth day, when, after the whipping, it died. To make complete his work, the captain, whip in hand, then called the child's mother to pick up the little body and throw it over the rail. She refused at first, but, tortured by the cat, she took up the child, walked to the ship's side, and turning her head away dropped the body into the sea.

Of the truth of the story there is no doubt. It was told under oath before a committee of Parliament, and of all the tales of inhuman deeds perpetrated by the slavers, none had more effect in ridding the earth of the traffic than this.

From one point of view the picture of a gang of slaves when on deck for an airing was one of the most shocking known to the trade. For the slaver captain knew how much brooding over their wrongs tended to promote disease, and his chief object in bringing them on deck was to cheer them. He wanted them to sing and dance, and he saw that they did it too—he applied the lash not only to make them eat, but to make them sing. There they stood in rows and as the brawny slaver, whip in hand, paced to and fro, they sang their home-songs, and danced, each with his free foot slapping the deck.

When the slaves tried to kill themselves because they believed in the resurrection and a life in their old homes after death, some of the slaver captains mutilated the bodies of the dead by cutting off and carrying along the heads or other portions of the bodies, and telling the slaves that thus the dead would be wholly unable to exist, or, at any rate, to enjoy the life they hoped for after death. But the slaves smiled in contempt when they heard that. They were of a heathen race. They had never learned the Christian's hope of heaven, but something had told them (who shall say how?) that the body, though it be "sown in corruption, it is raised in incorruption"— that though it be "sown a natural body, it is raised a spiritual body." And they—those heathen—trusted implicitly the light they had.

It is a most interesting fact that while the slave trade developed vikings when it was a legal and reputable traffic, it developed a race devoid of every manly instinct when it became unlawful. As illustrating this fact, it may be said that in the nineteenth century the slavers dealt in children as far as possible. Children did not bring as large a price as field hands, of course, but they cowered under torture, and there was no fear of their rising against the crew.

But many adult cargoes were shipped, and the American slaver *Kentucky*, Captain George H. Douglass, master, and Thomas H. Boyle, mate, was one that carried adults. On September 9, 1844, she sailed from Inhambane with five hundred and thirty slaves in her hold. On the voyage there was an insurrection. It was quickly subdued by force, but, through fear of more trouble of the kind, the captain determined to punish the ringleaders. In all, forty-six men and one woman were hanged and shot to death.

"They were ironed or chained, two together, and when they were hung, a rope was put round their necks and they drawn up to the yard-arm clear of the sail," said one of the crew when testifying under oath. "This did not kill them, but only choked or strangled them. They were then shot in the breast and the bodies thrown overboard. If only one of two that were ironed together was to be hung, the rope was put around his neck and he was drawn up clear of the deck, and his leg laid across the rail and chopped off to save the irons and release him from his companion, who at the same time lifted up his leg till the other was chopped off as aforesaid, and he released.

" The bleeding negro was then drawn up, shot in the breast, and thrown overboard as aforesaid. The legs of about one dozen were chopped off in this way.

" When the feet fell on deck they were picked up by the crew and thrown overboard, and sometimes they shot at the body while it still hung living, and all kinds of sport was made of the business.

" When the woman was hung up and shot, the ball did not take effect, and she was thrown overboard living, and was seen to struggle some time in the water before she sunk; and deponent further says, that after this was over they brought up and flogged about twenty men and six women. The flesh of some of them where they were flogged putrefied and came off in some cases six or eight inches in diameter, and in places half an inch thick."

This story, sworn to before United States Consul George William Gordon, was repeated by Consul Henry A. Wise (of Virginia) in an official communication to Secretary of State James Buchanan, under date of May 1, 1845. James K. Polk was then President of the United States, and this story and other stories of like character were sent to the Congress of the United States in House Ex. Doc. 61, 30th Congress second session, and Senate Ex. Doc. 28 of the same session.

Said Consul Wise in an official letter dated February 18, 1845:

"I beseech, I implore, the President of the United States to take a decided stand on this subject. You have no conception of the bold effrontery and the flagrant outrages of the African slave-trade, and of the shameless manner in which its worst crimes are licensed here. And every patriot in our land would blush for our country did he know and see, as I do, how *our own citizens sail and sell our flag* to the uses and abuses of that accursed traffic. We are a 'by-word among nations'—the only people who can now fetch and carry any and everything for the slave-trade . . . and, because we are the only people who can, are we to allow our proudest privilege to be perverted, and to pervert our own glorious flag into the *pirate's flag?* "

Neither James Buchanan nor James K. Polk, nor any other member of any administration from and including that of Andrew Jackson down to the Civil War, did anything that could in justice be called an effort to stop the use of the American flag for covering such atrocities.

It is a significant fact that there was one slave-ship named *Martin Van Buren* and another named *James Buchanan*. It is a pity that these two slavers could not have been preserved in the navy yard of the American metropolis as monuments to the officials whose names they bore, and to remind the shuddering spectator that along with our days of magnificent glory we have had our age of infinite shame.

CHAPTER VII

THE SLAVERS' PROFIT

Nine Hundred Pounds on One Voyage of the Newport Slaver *Sanderson*, a Vessel that was Offered for Sale at £450 with No Buyers—One Voyage of the Liverpool Slaver *Enterprise* that Paid £24,430—Details of Expenses and Receipts on a Voyage of the Ninety-ton Schooner *La Fortuna*—A Baltimore Schooner's Profit of $100,000—When the *Venus* Cleared $200,000—Sums Paid to Captains and Crews—Slave Transportation Compared with Modern Passenger Traffic.

IT has been repeatedly asserted in the course of this work that the slave-trade was, on the whole, enormously profitable, and it is now proposed to give in a business way some facts in verification of those assertions. There were, of course, many voyages that went awry, but that that was not the usual course of the trade is abundantly proved. Thus, the fact that Newport had one hundred and fifty vessels in the trade by the middle of the eighteenth century, shows what Newport merchants made out of the traffic. That Liverpool had but one sloop of thirty tons in the trade in 1729, while in 1751 "no fewer than fifty-three vessels, with an aggregate burthen of 5,334 tons, sailed from the Mersey for the slave-coast," shows how Liverpool slavers prospered. But something more than these general statements must prove of interest.

82

To go back to an early period, we find that the negroes imported on the *White Horse* (the first slaver sent out from New York for the direct trade with Africa) were sold at auction for an average price of $125 each for the choice stock. The negroes had arrived in a bad condition, but they were doctored up for the sale, and brought good prices for that day, so that the slaver made a good profit even though the purchasers afterward lost some of their slaves. The exact profit is not given, but the fact that a profit was made is proved by the act of the directors of the West India Company taking the trade thereafter into their own hands.

When Captain David Lindsay, of the *Sanderson*, sold the cargo he landed "in helth and fatt" in 1753 he received £35 each for twenty-five of his slaves, £30 each for three more, while the remainder brought prices ranging down to £21, save one small boy who brought £15. All told, forty-seven slaves sold here brought £1,432. The remaining slaves were carried to Newport, but there is no record of their sale. We may guess that they realized about £250, or, say, a total of £1,680 for the cargo of slaves.

The net profit on this voyage cannot be ascertained now, but Captain George Scott's letter of 1740 says that a prime slave cost £12 in the unsalable dry goods, while other documents show that in 1753 a prime slave cost one hundred and ten gallons of rum, or £11. The gross profit on the slaves sold in Barbadoes was doubtless as much as £900, and the net profit on the whole voyage, after the remaining slaves were sold elsewhere, was at least £900. And yet the *Sanderson* had been offered for sale several years earlier for £450, and during this voyage, as we have learned already, her captain was able to see "daylight al round" through the open seams in her bows.

In Williams's "Liverpool Slave Trade" it is shown that in 1786 the Liverpool slavers sold 31,690 slaves for £1,282,690 net. The gross value of the goods exported to Africa was £864,895, while the maintenance of the slaves cost £15,845. That leaves £401,950 for the owners of the slavers, from which, however, they had to pay their crews and the wear and tear of the ships. These expenses are classed as "freight," at £103,488, but the fact is there was a profit on the "freight." Nevertheless, calling the freight all expense, the clean profit was £298,462.

That is an estimate giving the expenses at the highest limit, and the sales at the lowest. Going more into detail, the returns for a single good voyage are given.

The ship *Lottery*, Captain John Whittle, belonged to Mr. Thomas Leyland, who was "thrice Mayor of Liverpool." She sailed from the Mersey on July 6, 1798, and passed Barbadoes on November 27th with four hundred and sixty negroes. Of these four hundred and fifty-three were sold for £22,726 net—the owner received that sum after paying all commissions and charges. From this sum, however, must be deducted £2,307 10s. for the ship's outfit and £8,326 14s. for the cost of the cargo sent out to Africa, a total of £10,634, which leaves the sum of £12,091 profit on the voyage. That is to say the profit on each negro was over £26, and it was earned in six months.

The *Lottery* in another voyage cleared £19,021. The *Enterprise* on a cargo of three hundred and ninety-two slaves landed, cleared £24,430. The *Fortune* on three hundred and forty-three cleared £9,487. The

Louisa on three hundred and twenty-six slaves cleared £19,133. The *Bloom*, belonging to another house, on three hundred and seven slaves cleared £8,123. An average of six voyages shows a clean profit of £43 per slave. And to this profit was added that on the West India goods carried to Liverpool when the ship went home to refit.

Other estimates of single voyages give profits ranging from £12 up to £40 per head landed.

An important element in the trade was the cost of the ship. The records show that a good ship fit to carry from three hundred to four hundred slaves could be built for £7,500. Such a ship would make a clean profit of from £7,000 to £20,000 each voyage, and it is certain that some of them made as high as five voyages before they became so foul that they had to be abandoned.

Of the profits made when the trade was declared to be piracy we have abundant records, even though it was a smuggling business.

Captain Theodore Canot in his autobiography, "Twenty Years of an African Slaver" (it is practically an autobiography), has the following (p. 101):

As the reader may scarcely credit so large a profit, I subjoin an account of the fitting of a slave vessel from Havana in 1827, and the liquidation of her voyage in Cuba:

1.—*Expenses Out.*

Cost of *La Fortuna*, a 90-ton schooner.... $3,700.00
Fitting out, sails, carpenter's and cooper's
    bills.................................... 2,500.00
Provisions for crew and slaves.......... 1,115.00
Wages advanced to 18 men before the mast   900.00

Wages advanced to captain, mates, boat-
swain, cook and steward............... 440.00
200,000 cigars and 500 doubloons, cargo . 10,900.00
Clearance and hush-money.............. 200.00
_____
Total............................$19,755.00
Commission at 5%..................... 987.00
_____
Full cost of voyage out $20,742.00

2.—*Expenses Home.*

Captain's head-money, at $8 a head...... $1,736.00
Mate's   "   "   " $4 " " 873.00
Second mate's and boatswain's head-
money, at $2 each 873.00
Captain's wages....................... 219.78
First mate's wages.................... 175.56
Second mate's and boatswain's wages..... 307.12
Cook's and steward's wages............ 264.00
18 sailors' wages 1,972.00
_____
Total of expenses out and home.......$27,162.46

3.—*Expenses in Havana.*

Government officers, at $8 per head...... $1,736.00
My commission on 217 slaves, expenses off 5,565.00
Consignees' commission 3,873.00
217 slave dresses 634.00
Extra expenses of all kinds 1,000.00
_____
Total of all expenses.................$39,970.46

4.—*Returns.*

Vessel at auction...................... $3,950.00
Proceeds of 217 slaves................. 77,469.00
_____
$81,419.00

Résumé.

Total Returns.....................$81,419.00
" Expenses...................... 39,970.46

Net Profit $41,448.54

With a schooner that cost $3,700 and a total capital all told, amounting to less than $21,000, the net profit in six months was $41,438.54.

Writing on the same subject, Captain Philip Drake tells about one voyage he made in the schooner *Napoleon*.

"The *Napoleon* was a ninety-ton Baltimore clipper, a model for speed and symmetry. She came out from Cuba, in ballast, as a new craft, and made two successful trips before, at Don Pedro's request, I supplied the place of mate and surgeon in her last voyage, when she sailed freighted with two hundred and fifty full-grown men and one hundred picked boys and girls for the Cuban market. By actual calculation the average cost per head of the three hundred and fifty was $16, and in Havana the market average was $360, yielding a profit for the whole, if safely delivered, at $360 a head, of $120,400 on the slaves. Subtracting $20,000 from this, the average cost of the clipper's round trip, including commissions, and her earnings would be $100,000 in round numbers. Such were the enormous profits of the slave-trade in 1835."

An official report on the first voyage of the beautiful Baltimore clipper ship *Venus* [See House Ex. Doc. 115, 26th Cong. 2d Sess.] says:

"With regard to the ship *Venus*, otherwise the *Duquesa de Braganza*, we should state that the original cost, we understand, was 30,000 dollars ; and that the fitting out, and expenses of every description for the voyage, including the value of the return cargo, was estimated at $60,000 more. The number of negroes brought back, as has been before stated, was 860 ; and they are said to have been sold at 340 dollars per head, producing the sum of nearly 300,000 dollars ; of which therefore two-thirds was net profit.'' That was in 1838-39.

As far back as 1827, the captain of a small slaver would receive $2,000 for a round trip requiring six months' time, while the mate got $1,000. To fully appreciate how much money that was to a ship's officers one has to remember that even now there are plenty of captains of schooners and barks of a thousand tons capacity who receive but $75 or $80 a month, although wages all around are fifty per cent. higher, and even more. The captains of transatlantic liners to-day receive from $2,000 to $3,000 a year, whereas the captain of a little ninety-ton slaver got $2,000 in six months. The liner that cost, say, a million dollars will carry first-class passengers in luxurious state-rooms and furnish abundant meals for from $100 to $150 for the passage, and $125 is a fair average price for superb accommodations on the most expensive vessel. The average profit on a slave after the year 1825 was not less than $250, or twice the price of a first-class passage on a ship costing a million. To make the contrast absolutely fair we should say that the slaver who received $340 per head, and paid but $20 in Africa received $320 for transporting the slave to Cuba. His net profit was reduced to, say, $250 by the expenses of the voyage, just as the steam liner's net profit may be reduced to $25 by the expenses of the voyage.

However, to be liberal, there was the sum of $250 net, at least, which the slaver could get for transporting a negro from Africa to Cuba. If the owners of steamships costing a million can afford to carry first-class passengers in luxury for $125, the slaver might have carried negroes in cleanliness and perfect comfort, and still have realized profits of from fifty to one hundred per centum every voyage, from the investment. It is plain that the horrors of the Middle Passage were not necessarily incident to the transportation of slaves from Africa to the West Indies.

CHAPTER VIII

SLAVER LEGISLATION IN THE AMERICAN COLONIES

The Colonies often Levied Taxes on Imported Slaves, and these Duties were in Rare Cases Prohibitive, but this Legislation was always Based on Commercial Considerations Only, or else a Fear of Negro Insurrections—Great Britain Never Forced the Slave-trade on Them Against Their Virtuous Protest—Georgia's Interesting Slave History.

IF there is any chapter in our history that is likely to make a patriotic student an utter pessimist, it is the chapter relating to American slave legislation. No other chapter is so disheartening ; none can excite such indignation and contempt. But if we consider that at last, after two hundred and forty-two years of oppression and robbery, a time came when we did, by legal enactment, recognize that a negro man was entitled at least to life, *liberty*, and the pursuit of happiness, we shall not be without hope that a time may yet come when we shall fully understand and act upon the Divine command, "Thou shalt love thy neighbor as thy self."

That the British Government, in the interest of British shipping, did, in the eighteenth century, try to encourage the slave-trade is abundantly proved by many other facts than the appropriations, amounting to £90,000, which Parliament granted, between 1729 and 1750, for building, repairing, and supporting forts and

slave-pens on the coast of Africa. But whether the
American colonies *virtuously* struggled to resist and
suppress the slave-traffic during those years is another
matter entirely.

To begin with the facts in the matter, we find that in
New York in 1709 a tariff duty of £3 per head was laid
on all negroes *imported from any other place than an
African port*, and this is said to have been prohibitive.

In connection with this take the letter of the Earl of
Bellemont to the Lords of Trade:

" I should advise the sending for negroes to Guinea,
which I understand are bought there and brought
hither, all charges whatever being bourne, for £10 a
piece, New York money. . . . If it were practical
for the King to be the merchant and that the whole
management of this undertaking were upon his account, were it so, there would be profit of at least £50
per cent." (Vol. IV. Col. Doc.)

The tax was laid to promote a direct trade   In 1716
a tariff then imposed was explained by Governor
Hunter. (Vol. V., N. Y. Col. Doc.)

"The duties laid on negroes from ye other colonies
are intended *to encourage their own shipping* and dis-
courage their importing of refuse and sickly negroes
here from other colonies, which they commonly do."

The fact is that while New York State eventually
abolished slavery, it never put so much as a spray of
sea-weed under the bows of slave-ships owned by her
citizens.

In Rhode Island, as early as 1708, a tax of £3 per
head was laid on all negroes imported. This tax has
been called a restraint on the trade and it has been
quoted to show that the Rhode Islanders even thus

early showed a glimmering sense of the moral character of the slave-trade. The fact is the tax was laid to enable the Colonial Government to obtain a share of the profits of the trade, and Newport streets were first paved out of the proceeds of that tax.

Moore, in his " Slavery in Massachusetts," points out that in 1701 the representatives from Boston were " desired [by the voters] to promote the encouraging the bringing of white servants, and to put a period to negroes being slaves." That looks like a real desire to abolish slavery, even though no legislation followed on the desire ; but the truth is, the Boston voters were animated solely by business principles, as shall be pointed out in connection with similar legislation in New Jersey.

Moreover " the law of 1703 (two years later) chapter 2, was in restraint of the ' Manumission, Discharge or Setting free ' of ' Molatto or Negro slaves.' " The close-fisted slave-owners had begun " to manumit aged or infirm slaves, to relieve the master from the charge of supporting them."

In 1705 Massachusetts again enacted slaver laws. One clause of the bill imposed a tax of £4 on each slave imported. This looks something like a restraint of the trade, but a further examination of the act shows that it was " for the Better Preventing of a spurious or mixt Issue." It is shocking to learn that the young men of Puritan blood were so fond of the black Briseises. Another clause of the bill provided for an entire rebate of the tax if the slaves were exported after having been entered at the custom house. The act was really designed to enable the colony to share in the profits of the slave-trade, and to encourage slavers in making Boston a clearing-house, so to speak, for the slave-trade of the whole continent.

Du Bois notes that the middle colony and southern ports allowed a rebate of not more than one-half the duty of reshipment of slaves; but the student must not fail to consider this in its proper light. It was not a question of morals—of a desire to suppress the slave-trade. The middle and southern ports were merely less anxious to promote sea-traffic—they were less under the influence of ship-owners.

It appears that New Jersey really strove to prohibit the trade in 1713, by a duty of £10. This law looks quite a little like an honest attempt to extirpate the traffic. It certainly was not the expression of a desire to participate in the profits, or to promote shipping, or to interfere with the trade of other colonies. But on looking at the real reason we find (Vol. IV. New Jersey Archives) that it was "calculated to Encourage the Importation of white Servants for the better Peopeling that Country."

It was seen clearly in New Jersey, and also in other colonies (though dimly in some of them) that white servants of a character to become enterprising citizens, when their term of slavery was ended, were likely to be of more benefit to a community with a climate like that of any of the northern colonies than African slaves would be. The negro was to be a slave for life —a mere laborer whose value was as that of a horse. But a large proportion of the white slaves became, at last, business men who would develop the natural resources of the country, and build the nation.

And all this is to say, with emphasis, that the prohibitive legislation of New Jersey, as of some other communities, was based strictly on *business* considerations. The only question really was, Which in the end will pay best—white or black servants?

In Pennsylvania the first law to impose a prohibitive tax was passed in 1712, and the bill itself sets forth the object in view. It began: "Whereas divers Plots and Insurrections have frequently happened, not only in the Islands, but on the Mainland of *America*, by Negroes, which have been carried on so far that several of the inhabitants have been barbarously Murthered, an Instance whereof we have lately had in our Neighboring Colony of *New York*," etc. The act ended by imposing a duty of £20.

For fear the slaves whom they dominated might rise to secure liberty and avenge uncounted injuries, the people of Pennsylvania decided that no more slaves should come in. It was the sheer cowardice of conscious tyrants that animated those Pennsylvania legislators.

A similar state of affairs was developed in South Carolina very early—in 1698—when it was said that "the great number of negroes which of late have been imported into this collony may endanger the safety thereof," and a special law to encourage the importation of white servants was passed. A few years later, when the King of Spain and the Queen of England went into the slave-trade in partnership, heavy duties were laid on imported negroes, because "the number of Negroes do extremely increase," and "*the safety of the said Province* is greatly endangered." In 1717 a duty of £40 currency was laid, and this cut down importations so much that a duty of £10 was substi-

tuted for all others in 1719. In 1734 there were 22,000
slaves to less than 8,000 whites in South Carolina, and
this state of affairs was exceedingly alarming to the
whites, especially as insurrections had been attempted.

An insurrection at Stono under a negro called Cato
led to a prohibitive duty of £100 laid for a time on
imported negroes. Again in 1760 the importation was
prohibited through fear.

Georgia was first established by charitable English-
men as a refuge for a lot of people who were imprisoned for debt — in trouble through misfortune
only. The charter was granted June 9, 1732. It was
to be "a silk, wine, oil and drug growing colony."
And negro slavery was absolutely prohibited.

T. Rundle, one of the trustees of the corporation, in
a sermon preached at St. George's, February 17, 1733,
said : "Let avarice defend it as it will, there is an
honest reluctance in humanity against buying and
selling, and regarding those of our own species as
our wealth and possessions." To this Oglethorpe
himself, the colony's chief promoter, added that the
slave-trade was "against the gospel as well as the
fundamental law of England," and that "we refused
as Trustees to make a law permitting such a horrid
crime."

In view of the regulations covering rum and negro
slaves, Du Bois, the distinguished historian of the
negro race, is moved to say that "in Georgia we have
an example of a community whose philanthropic
founders sought to impose upon it a code of morals
higher than the colonists wished."

The fact is, however, that Oglethorpe was Deputy
Governor of the Royal African Company, the company

chartered to monopolize the slave-trade under the famous Assiento contract with Spain—the company which agreed to deliver 4,800 slaves per year, or 144,000 slaves in all, in the Spanish colonies alone, during the course of thirty years, and which did deliver many more than 4,800 slaves into the American colonies in the very year when Oglethorpe made a speech on the slave-trade declaring it a "horrid crime." He also owned a plantation near Parachucla, South Carolina, forty miles north of the Savannah River, that was worked by slaves. Oglethorpe proclaimed (as many an American did after him) that the slave-trade was "horrid," but he was one of the most active participants in it known to his age. The conclusion reached by Stevens in his "History of Georgia" is irresistible. "It was policy and not philanthropy which prohibited slavery" in the settlement of Georgia. The policy was the desire to place a buffer—perhaps one should rather say a sentinel troop—between the Spanish forces of Florida and the English colony of Carolina. The Carolina people felt that their slaves were an element of great weakness should the Spanish come as invaders. A colony of white men only would serve as an outpost that the Spaniards would fear and respect.

But Georgia did not prosper as a settlement of whites only, and slaves were, at last, introduced, at the urgent demand of the colonists.

To omit further details of colonial policy it may be said generally that, with the exception of Georgia, every colony did at one time and another impose taxes on imported negro slaves, and that in some cases the so-called restraint amounted to prohibition.

HE APPLIED THE LASH NOT ONLY TO MAKE THEM EAT BUT TO MAKE THEM SING.

See page 78.

But with this admission it must be declared that every such tax was laid either through greed (*i.e.*, for the sake of giving the State a share of the profits) or through the idea that from a business point of view white servants would develop the country more rapidly ; or through a mean and degrading fear of the blacks. Not one act passed by a colonial legislature showed any appreciation of the intrinsic evil in the trade or tended to extirpate it from the seas—not one. It might as well be asserted that our present tariff on imported woollen goods shows that we abhor shepherds and desire to extirpate the world's traffic in wool, as to assert that the colonial tariffs on the slave-trade were honest efforts to rid the world of a horrid traffic. The world was not at that time sufficiently civilized to even discuss the rights of slaves. It was not until 1772 that Granville Sharp, the lone abolitionist of England, got one lone question regarding one right of one lone slave heard and decided in an English court. The assertion that the British forced the traffic on unwilling colonists in America is a puling whine.

CHAPTER IX

THE EARLY WORK FOR EXTIRPATION

The Words and Deeds of the Fanatics—The Quakers—Slaves that were Freed by Baptism—Granville Sharp as a Liberator—A Fanatic's Political Creed Plainly Stated—Widespread Influence of the Somerset Case when the Right Prevailed in England—A Policy that would not Square Well with a Practical Business Sense of Things—The American Declaration of Independence and the Black Men.

WHEN Sir John Hawkins, flushed with success, was telling Good Queen Bess how he had taken, "partly by the sword and partly by other means" three hundred negroes from the coast of Guinea to the far side of the Atlantic and sold them there with profit, the heart of the Queen was touched and she saw, back of the "great profit," the picture of the negroes when they were torn from their homes by force, and she said the deed "was detestable." For one brief moment she saw clear-eyed, and a writer recorded her words where they were most likely to find readers among her people—in a naval history.

The importance of the fact that her words were printed is to be emphasized. The reader will recall what Carlyle says of the voiceless millions, whose sufferings made the French revolution possible, in contrast with the screaming outcries of the few who were unjustly treated therein while those millions held power. When the protest of Elizabeth was printed, the voiceless negro slave was heard.

In like fashion the slave was heard again when Morgan Godwyn, a clergyman employed by the slaveholding missionary society of England, wrote "The Negroes' and Indians' Advocate." Then Richard Baxter wrote a "Christian Directory," wherein he gives "advice to those masters in foreign plantations who have negroes and other slaves."

They were sowing good seed—a sort of winterwheat crop, one may say. The Pennsylvania Quakers took up the work and on "the 13th day of the 8th month, 1693," at "our Monthly Meeting in Philadelphia," prepared an "Exhortation and Caution to Friends Concerning Buying or Keeping of Negroes."

They were opposed to "keeping negroes for Term of Life" for several reasons clearly stated, the "fifthly" of which shall be quoted: "Because slaves and souls of men are some of the *Merchandize of Babylon*, by which the Merchants of the Earth are made Rich."

In the valuable and interesting book called "The Workers" by Walter A. Wyckoff, is a graphic description of the effect, as he observed it, of a sermon upon a wealthy congregation in a Chicago church which he attended that he might see how a laborer would be received among the wealthy. So earnest was the preacher, so intent were the audience, that (to quote the author) "it was as though distress had ceased to be for them the visible sufferings of the poor, and had grown, through the deepening sense of brotherhood, into an anguish of their own, which must find

healing in forms of effective helpfulness. Very clearly
dawned the conviction that, if one could but point out
to the members of this waiting company some 'way,'
' something to do, which *would square well with their
practical business sense* of things, instant and un-
measured would be their response.' "

The quotation emphasizes the work of the Quakers
of 1693, for they did not ask nor did they so much as
think of what would square with practical business
sense.   There is not a word in their manifesto, nor was
there a thought in the heart of one of them, about the
"*Impolicy* of the Slave-trade."   And they were followed by many others who refused to entertain *business* considerations, but asked solely what was right.

The story of the Boston slaver, who, in 1645, robbed
an African village by force of arms of its inhabitants,
was told in open court because the slaver captain quarrelled with the ship's owners.   On hearing it, one of the
magistrates, Richard Saltonstall, declared that the
master and his mate had been guilty of murder, man-
stealing, and Sabbath-breaking, *all crimes* " *capital
by the law of God.*"   This was the first time that a
man was accused in open court, on United States soil,
of a capital offence because he had stolen negroes in
Africa.   It was the first of the long series of slave-
trials wherein the insolent slaver was let go on techni-
calities, the Courts deciding that they had no jurisdiction over crimes committed by citizens of the colony
when on the coast of Africa.

The next court case worth mention here came up
in 1767.   In 1727 the British planters of the West
Indies who came to England bringing slaves for
personal attendants began to have trouble through

the efforts of the slaves to escape service. The negroes, seeing the relative freedom and comfort of the white servants of England, ran away. For a time the masters had merely to find the negroes to recover them, but eventually it was noised among the negroes that, under the laws of England, every human being who had been baptized in the Established Church was free. Thereat every negro made haste to get baptized.

The law was plain in letter and spirit, but the Crown Attorney and the Solicitor-General, at the request of certain slave-owners, wrote an opinion saying that baptism of a slave could not divest the slave-owner of any property right. That opinion served as law for nearly forty years.

But in 1765 a Barbadoes planter named David Lisle came to London bringing a negro slave named Jonathan Strong with him, and took lodgings in Wapping. Lisle abused Strong in shocking fashion and then turned him into the street, as he would have turned a worthless dog, to die.

At that time a Dr. William Sharp lived in Wapping, and he gave much time to charity. In some way the negro Strong found his way to Sharp's office. Sharp heard his story and sent him to a hospital, where he was cured. Now, Dr. Sharp had a brother, one Granville Sharp, "born at Durham, England, November 10, 1735. His early education was limited. In 1750 he was apprenticed to a *Friend*—afterward to an Independent—and subsequently to a Romanist." The story of the negro Strong appealed to Granville, who after he left the hospital obtained a situation for him where all went well with him until one day in 1767 his old master saw him, and at once decided to take possession of him again. To this end he had the slave kidnapped, and then sold him to one John Kerr for £30.

Although held in prison, Strong found means to send for friends, and Granville Sharp went to the Lord Mayor, Sir Robert Kite, "and entreated him to send for Strong, and to hear his case."

Accordingly the case was heard, and Strong was discharged from custody on the ground that he had been kidnapped—that is, really, on a technical plea. Sharp freed Strong, but this case established no principle worth mention, and the story is told chiefly because the work of Sharp in the case was his first effort in behalf of the negro race, and great things were to follow through his later efforts.

Straightway Sharp found his hands full of the work of liberating slaves. So let us look his work in the face. It was nothing more nor less than an attack on property legally obtained and legally held. It was a work that would not "square with the business sense" of anybody. It is, therefore, but justice to the man to let him say here what the faith was that moved him to this extraordinary career. In a letter to Lord Carysport he said:

"This is the compendium or sum total of all my politics, so that I include them in a very small compass. I am thoroughly convinced that *Right* ought to be adopted and maintained, on all occasions, *without regard to consequences either probable or possible.*"

This was the first statement made by an abolitionist of what the abolitionists called "the higher law."

In November, 1769, Charles Stewart, a Virginia planter, brought a slave named James Somerset to

England. Somerset ran away ; was recaptured, and was placed on the ship *Mary and Ann* to be carried to Jamaica and sold. On learning this fact Sharp took the negro from the ship on the usual writ, and it was agreed that the case should turn on the broad question "Whether an African slave coming into England becomes free."

That was a trial to stir the kingdom, for it was an open attack not alone on the planters of distant colonies, but on the whole foreign commerce of the nation that had been developed, nurtured, improved, and brought to the leading place on the sea through the profits of the slave-trade. Worse yet, from a business point of view, it was an attack upon many interests ashore. The distilleries that made rum, the factories that made ropes, sails, and other ship fittings, even the whole industry of Manchester that turned out cloths for the African trade — all these were interested in the success of the slavers.

The wealth of the nation and the power of society gathered on one side. On the other side stood a timorous negro slave and Granville Sharp. Lord Mansfield in his robes presided.

For six months—from January to June, 1772, inclusive—blind Justice held the scales aloft in that court while learned counsel heaped this side and that with lore and statute bald, and strove with fierce as well as pleading breath to sway the poised beam. And then he who stood for the oppressed, rising above the obscuring, tape-bound "chaos of formulas," asked in a voice that was heard in spite of clamor:

"Shall the Right prevail in England?"

When those words were heard a hush fell upon all

in that court, as if God had spoken. And then Justice raised her sword, and, while the timorous slave and the arrogant master listened, the justice who was appointed to speak said :

"Immemorial usage preserves the memory of positive law long after all traces of the occasion, reason, authority, and time of its introduction are lost ; and in a case so odious as that of the condition of slaves, must be taken strictly (tracing the subject to natural principles, the claim of slavery never can be supported). The power claimed by this return never was in use here. We cannot say the cause set forth by this return is allowed or approved of by the laws of this kingdom, and therefore the man must be discharged."

That was said on Monday, June 22, 1772. From that day slave-traders lost England as a landing-place —lost her waters even as ports of call while their human cargoes were on board. The slave-trade had been actually restricted regardless of business considerations.

Not only did the case of Somerset serve to restrict the territory of the slave-traders ; the stir it created in public talk was of tremendous effect. For it should be recalled that under the laws of England and of the colonies in those days it was libellous to tell the truth in public print about the ill-treatment a slave might receive from his master, unless, indeed, the story of it were first told in open court during a trial involving the matter. The cases which Granville Sharp brought into court enabled the masses of the English-speaking people who held no slaves to learn lawfully how slaves were treated by slave-owners, and this set them to considering whether or not slave-owning was right.

Granville Sharp, in fighting the battle of an unfortunate negro, prepared the way in England for the discussion of slavery and the slave-trade on their merits. The voiceless negro through him appealed to the justice and humanity of the dominant race.

In America no such appeal as that was heard, but a demand was made there for universal liberty, and it was heard around the world because emphasized by the thunder of cannon.

When the colonists united to oppose British oppression, the talk about slavery and slaves, which had reference to their own condition, turned their thoughts to the unfortunate negro slaves, and on Thursday, October 20, 1774, they signed an agreement that they would "not purchase any slave imported after the first day of December next; after which time we will wholly discontinue the slave-trade, and will neither be concerned in it ourselves, nor will we hire our vessels, nor sell our commodities or manufactures to those who are concerned in it."

CHAPTER X

THE SLAVERS OUTLAWED

British Abolitionists and Their Work—After a Crusade of only
Twenty Years, They Outlawed a Trade that, from a Busi-
ness Point of View, had been the most Profitable in the
United Kingdom—The Slave-trade and the American
Constitution—Inauguration of the System of Compromises
that Led to the Civil War—Slave-trade Legislation of the
States—The Act of March 2, 1807.

ALTHOUGH the British - American colonies, from
Massachusetts to Georgia, had become the United
States of America before anything was done through
a love of humanity for the legal abolition of the traffic,
it is necessary, for the purposes of this history, to consider the progress of the trade, and of its opponents,
very much as if no separation had taken place between the colonies and the mother country.

Although the notable decision that right should
prevail in England, as far as the negro Somerset was
concerned, was made in 1772, it was not until 1787
that a "Society for the Abolition of the African Slave-
trade," was formed in London. However, an abolition association, or committee without special organization, was formed as early as 1783. The immediate
cause of its formation was the story of the slaver
Zong already related.

The first meeting of the committee was held July 7,

1783, "to consider what steps they should take for the relief and liberation of the Negro slaves in the West Indies, and for the discouragement of the Slave-trade on the coast of Africa." The result of the agitation of this private committee was the formation on May 22, 1787, of the "Society for the Abolition of the African Slave-trade," of which Granville Sharp was the chairman, and Thomas Clarkson was, next to Sharp, the most active member. In Parliament William Wilberforce became the champion of the society, chiefly through the work of Clarkson. Of the standing of the supporters of the trade we have a sufficient indication in the fact that their leader was His Royal Highness the Duke of Clarence, afterward William IV.

How the society held meetings and published appeals, and how the slavers were forced to reply but failed to show convincing arguments, cannot be told here. But in the meantime David Hartley, a member of Parliament from Hull, made a motion in the House, in 1776, "That the slave-trade is contrary to the laws of God and the rights of man." In support of this resolution he laid on the table of the House some of the irons used in securing slaves on the slave-ships. Sir George Saville seconded the motion, but, of course, it failed even of a respectful hearing.

In 1783 an effort was made to regulate the slave-trade, and it was then the abolition committee began its work. The bill of 1783 failed, but because of the continually increasing agitation by the abolitionists "the King by an order in council, dated February 11th, 1788, directed that a committee of the Privy Council should sit as a board of trade 'to take into their consideration the present state of the African trade, particularly as far as related to the practice and manner of purchasing or obtaining slaves on the coast of Africa, and the importation or sale thereof' " in the markets of the West.

On May 9, 1788, the first real discussion of the slave trade was heard in Parliament. Mr. Pitt moved a resolution to the effect that a full discussion of the trade be had in the next session, and his motion prevailed.

However, Sir William Dolben was not satisfied to allow the session to close without doing something to relieve the slaves, and on May 21, 1788, asked leave to bring in a bill which was designed " only to limit the number of persons to be put on board to the tonnage of the vessel which was to carry them, in order to prevent them from being crowded too closely together ; to secure them good and sufficient provisions, and to take cognizance of other matters which related to their health and accommodation ; and this only till Parliament could enter into the general merits of the question."

The slavers at once protested that any restriction would ruin the trade, but meantime Mr. Pitt had sent Captain Parry, of the Royal Navy, to Liverpool to measure the slavers there, and his measurements showed that many slavers had made enormous profits where fewer slaves had been carried than the contemplated bill would permit. It was now that the people learned how little space was allowed to the slaves crowded into the slaver's hold.

On June 17, 1788, the bill passed the House of Commons by a vote of fifty-six to five. By its terms slavers were to be allowed to carry " five men to every three tons in every ship under one hundred and fifty tons burthen [according to the custom-house measurement] which had the space of five feet between the decks, and three men to two tons in every vessel beyond one hundred and fifty tons which had equal accommodation in point of height between the decks."

In the House of Lords, in spite of increased opposition, the bill was amended to compel the carrying of regularly educated surgeons on every slaver and to give bounties to slaver captains who lost no more than two per centum of the slaves during the Middle Passage. Finally, on Thursday, July 10, 1788, "the first bill that ever put fetters upon that barbarous and destructive monster, The Slave-trade," was sent to the King. And on the next day the King signed it and it became the law of the realm.

The Parliamentary investigation of the trade followed, and this gave the public a full knowledge of its horrors. As already said, these horrors grew up only because of the blind greed of the slavers. They might perhaps, by giving the slaves good passenger accommodations, have long delayed the fate that was at hand. But blind they were. On April 27, 1792, Parliament passed a resolution by a vote of one hundred and fifty-one to one hundred and thirty-two for the abolition of the trade in 1796. In the House of Lords it failed.

In 1793 the abolitionists failed in the Commons as well as the House of Lords. In 1794 the measure was carried in the Commons but lost in the upper house. Then an effort was made to keep British ships from supplying foreigners, and that failed. A supreme effort seems to have been made in 1799, but that failed also, and thereafter nothing of importance was done in

Parliament until 1804, which was fixed upon for re-
newed exertions. A bill then passed the Commons,
but was thrown out by the Lords.

However, in 1805 " an order in council prohibited the
importation of negroes to the newly conquered colonies of the British Crown." Following this "Sir A.
Pigott, the Attorney-General, as an officer of the
Crown, brought in a bill on March 31, 1806, the first
object of which was to give effect" to that order. The
second object was "to prohibit British subjects from
being engaged in importing slaves into the colonies of
any foreign power." A third object was "to prohibit
British subjects and British capital from being employed in carrying on a slave-trade in foreign ships,"
and to prevent foreign slavers fitting out in British
ports. This bill, "the first which dismembered this
cruel trade," passed the Commons at once, and the
Lords on May 7th, when it was signed by the King.
The triumph of Humanity was at hand. Parliament
was dissolved in November, 1806, but public opinion
had so far changed that Roscoe, a noted abolitionist,
could be sent from Liverpool, the chief slaver port,
to the new Parliament that was soon convened. It
was a short-lived Parliament, but a bill was passed
declaring that no vessel should clear out for slaves
from any port within the British dominions after May
1, 1807, and that no slave should be landed in the colonies after March 1, 1808. It received the King's signa-
ture on March 25, 1807. The fight that was organized
in 1787, when the abolitionists formed their society for
outlawing the trade, was won.

This was not the first time that the trade had been
prohibited by legal enactment in an English-speaking

state, but it was the first time such a law had been made from humane motives only.

To consider the course of events on our side of the Atlantic, it appears that "the slave-trade was hardly touched upon in the Congress of the Confederation." It was mentioned only in connection with "the counting of slaves as well as of freemen in the apportionment of taxes;" but when the articles were finally adopted a law was enacted by which fugitive slaves, captured on the sea, or on the beach below high-water mark, were to be free unless claimed by the owner!

From the adoption of the articles of confederation until it was found that those articles were utterly inadequate to their proposed object of holding the States together as a nation, the slave-trade was not an object of national legislation. But when the convention which adopted the present Constitution met, the subject of the slave-trade had a fair discussion, though it must be said that no one foresaw the extent to which slavery was to grow. On the contrary, the people as a whole believed that it was a dying institution, destined speedily to take itself from the nation.

A fair examination of the discussions in this convention shows that the trade would have been prohibited in the Constitution but for the delegates from Georgia and South Carolina. Delegates from Delaware, Maryland, and Virginia all denounced the traffic, even though all of them were slave-holders. Mason, of Virginia, called it "infernal." Georgia was ruled by the feeling in favor of slavery that had come down from the days when her financial interests had suffered for want of slaves under the proprietary government.

In South Carolina the people were probably influenced chiefly by what may be called the States' rights doctrine. They did not then need imported slaves. In fact, of their own will, they prohibited the traffic temporarily afterward. It was, apparently, the principle of surrendering the control of the trade to the general government to which they objected.

When the two States refused to join the confederacy, if the slave-trade were definitely prohibited, Roger Sherman, of Connecticut, said : "It is better to let the Southern States import slaves than to part with those States."

Herein was laid the foundation of the national legislation on slavery that was continued until it culminated in the civil war. It is certain that but for the compromises then inaugurated we should have had two nations instead of one formed from the original colonies.

In view of this undisputed fact, and in view of the history of the nation since that date, what does the reader think of the assertion of principle made by Granville Sharp, when he said:

"Right ought to be adopted and maintained on all occasions, without regard to consequences, either probable or possible ?"

And here let it be remembered that the slave question was discussed in the Constitutional Convention chiefly from an "economic standpoint," and that the word "slave"was carefully excluded from the instrument *for the sake of appearance.*

Not to dwell too long on a topic that is humiliating to every patriot, we find that the slave-trade matter was disposed of as follows in the Constitution :

ARTICLE I. SECTION 9. The Migration or Importation of such Persons as any of the States now existing shall think proper to admit shall not be prohibited by the Congress prior to the Year one thousand, eight hundred and eight, but a Tax or duty may be imposed on such Importation, not exceeding ten dollars for each Person.

The opponents of the trade provided for a date when the trade might be prohibited, and they saw that a negro was described as a "Person," not as an animal or real estate. This was something. People had been found to deny that a negro was a man and a brother, though the fact that he was a half-brother to some of the leading white citizens of the nation was patent enough.

Meantime the States were able, both under the confederation and under the Constitution, to deal with the slave-trade and slavery as they pleased. The State legislation was based chiefly on economic considerations, but the effect of the Declaration of Independence is also seen. New York, as a State, appears to have taken the lead in prohibitory legislation. On February 28, 1788, she enacted that no slave should be imported within her boundaries, nor should any be purchased in the State for export. The penalty was £100.

Massachusetts followed, on March 25, 1788, and prohibited to her citizens the African slave-trade. There was nothing in the act to prevent carrying slaves from any other continent.

Pennsylvania four days later was more sweeping, for

8

it prohibited the trade "to, from, or between Europe, Asia, Africa, or America, or any places or countries whatever."

South Carolina, during this year, prohibited the trade for a period (until January 1, 1793). Delaware followed with prohibition on February 3, 1789.

On May 13, 1789, it was proposed in Congress to tax the importation of slaves at $10 a head. The national government needed money badly, but this proposal to share in the profits of the trade was never carried.

The first real step toward a national restriction of the trade under the Constitution was taken on March 23, 1790. The abolitionists had been stirring up the menagerie—if one may be allowed the only term graphically descriptive of the members in their ordinary motives and doings in connection with disagreeable topics. Petition after petition on the subject of slavery and the trade had been sent in, and Congress had continued the policy of evasion inaugurated at the Constitutional Convention. But on that date the House declared "that Congress have authority to restrain the citizens of the United States from carrying on the African trade, for the purpose of supplying foreigners with slaves, and of providing, by proper regulations, for the humane treatment, during their passage, of slaves imported by the said citizens into the States admitting such importations." Further, "that Congress have authority to prohibit foreigners from fitting out vessels in any port of the United States for transporting persons from Africa to any foreign port."

The vote was twenty-nine to twenty-five, and even that was obtained only because the same resolutions declared that "Congress have no authority to interfere in the emancipation of slaves, or in the treatment of them within the States," and that "the migration or importation of such persons as any of the States now existing shall think proper to admit cannot be prohibited by Congress prior to the year one thousand, eight hundred and eight."

Four years passed before anything was done under these declared powers. The ills of the slave-trade as described by the witnesses before the English Parliament became widely known in this country, and the abolitionists, led by the persistent Quakers, kept nagging Congress with petitions for the abolition of slavery, but Congress went on, brushing these aside, until the shadow of the storm raised in Hayti by Toussaint L'Ouverture darkened the southern horizon. The slaves of the great island just east of Cuba arose, and in a day, so to speak, had asserted and maintained the principle that all men are born free and equal. Their rising, like that of the oppressed in France, was marked with the violence that power suddenly released from restraint always shows. Many and frightful were the deeds of bloodshed and rapine, and the thought of these and of the real cause of them made the white American legislators cower.

"A Quaker petition for a law against the transport traffic in slaves was received without a murmur in 1794, and on March 22 of that year the first national act against the slave-trade became a law."

The student finds, as he reads through the great mass of American works on slavery printed since that day, that many of the writers announce, with a flourish of Old Glory, that the United States was the first nation to prohibit the slave-trade. They think this act prohibited the trade.

The truth is the act was merely "to prohibit the carrying on the Slave-trade *from the United States to any foreign place or country*" and to prohibit fitting out slavers here for a foreign country. It was merely an act in mild restraint of the trade—so mild, in fact, that it never injured the slavers to the extent of a dollar.

Here the matter rested for six years—save only that by the act of April 3, 1798, "in relation to the Mississippi territory," to which the constitutional provision did not extend, the introduction of slaves was forbidden, under severe penalties, and every slave imported contrary to the act was to be entitled to freedom. But in 1800 a petition of Pennsylvania free negroes for a revision of the laws relating to the slave-trade, the fugitive slave law, and for gradual emancipation, once more stirred the House to fever heat.

In the debate that followed, Dana, of Connecticut, declared that the petition contained "nothing but a farrago of the French metaphysics of liberty and equality." That from Connecticut!

Brown, of Rhode Island, said: "We want money; we want a navy; we ought therefore to use the means to obtain it. . . . Why should we see Great Britain getting all the slave-trade to themselves—why may not our country be enriched by that lucrative traffic?"

Congress, however, made it unlawful not only to fit out ships for the foreign slave-trade but to hold any interest, direct or indirect, in foreign slaver voyages. And serving on slavers was prohibited to American citizens. Naval vessels were directed to make prizes of any American slave-ships, and the guilty merchants and crews were to bear, on conviction, an imprisonment of two years as well as a fine of $2,000 for a maximum penalty. The slaves were to be forfeited, but what was to be done with them was not said, although the captors were not to have them.

It was still lawful to import slaves from Africa into any State permitting the trade. On February 28, 1803, a bill became a law which provided for the forfeiture of any ship that should bring into any State, contrary to its laws, "any negro, mulatto, or other person of color." The ship-master violating this law was to be fined $1,000. Curiously enough, this law was passed on presentation of a petition from North Carolina. Some Haytian negroes had landed at Wilmington, and the North Carolinians were frightened by the thought that the Haytians were emissaries come to preach the Haytian ideas of liberty and equality.

Nevertheless the great profits in cotton planting, after Whitney invented the cotton gin, and was robbed of his rights, caused a reaction in favor of the slave-trade. To obtain more negroes for the cotton-field, South Carolina repealed her law prohibiting slave imports. What South Carolina did openly, other States did sneakingly; they smuggled slaves.

About that time the Louisiana Territory was under consideration in Congress, and many slaves were wanted there. Harper, of South Carolina, got a bill passed compelling the planters in Louisiana to import through "the limits of the United States;" the practical effect of the law being to make all slavers enter their cargoes at Charleston, after which they were at liberty to proceed to New Orleans.

As a result of this opening of the traffic in South Carolina, two hundred and two ships brought 39,075 slaves from Africa to Charleston during the years 1804 to 1807, inclusive. According to the official returns of the custom house as gathered by Senator Smith, of that State, and reported to Congress, these ships were divided as follows : " From Connecticut, 1 ; Boston, 1 ; Norfolk, 2 ; Baltimore, 4 ; Rhode Island, 59 ; Charleston, 61 ; Sweden, 1 ; France, 3 ; Great Britain, 70." There were only sixty-one ships nominally hailing from Northern ports engaged in the trade. But when one looks to see who reaped the profits, it appears that of the consignees of these slavers "88 were natives of Rhode Island, 13 of Charleston, 10 of France, and 91 of Great Britain."

Rhode Island passed in October, 1787, an act to prevent the importation of slaves into her own territory and to encourage the abolition of slavery in the State. Importation of slaves was prohibited under penalty of a fine of £100 per negro, and £1,000 per ship, but there was nothing in her legislation, or in any other legislation then extant, to prevent her shipowners reaping the profits of the open trade to South Carolina. It was right hard work to induce legislators in those days to shut off absolutely a business wherein a man could make $90,000 profit in one round voyage of a ship worth less than $10,000.

However, as the year 1808 drew nigh, legislation of importance was had. Congress had assumed that it had the right to prohibit the trade beginning with that year, and President Jefferson in his message of December 2, 1806, congratulated Congress " on the approach of the period at which you may interpose your authority constitutionally " to prohibit the slave-trade. The next day—December 3—Bradley, of Vermont, introduced the bill that became the act of March 2, 1807.

The first part of it considered was the disposal of the slaves in vessels to be captured while attempting to bring slaves in—that the ship-owners would violate the law was taken as a matter of course. The anti-slavery men wanted the negroes so captured to be free, but were willing to have them indentured, even for life. This was asking more than could be obtained. The fear of having free blacks turned loose in slave-holding communities—the fear that the free blacks would incite insurrections was too strong.

Of course there were moral objections to selling the slaves, but Congressman Joseph Clay declared "morality has nothing to do with this traffic. It must appear to every man of common-sense that the question can be considered in a commercial point of view only." Worse yet, Congressmen were found to argue for the "decent appearance" of the statute book. They were drabs who feared detection, not the sin.

Of course, in the state of civilization then prevailing the commercial consideration necessarily prevailed. The law (section 4), as at last passed, provided that "neither the importer, nor any person or persons claiming under him, shall hold any right or title whatsoever" to any negro which might be captured on a slaver coming to the United States, "but the same shall remain subject to any regulations," not contrary to this act, which "the several States or Territories" might make in the matter.

So Congress in trying to stop the traffic provided

that the unfortunates brought from Africa should not
regain the liberty they had lost through the work of
land pirates.

No slaves were smuggled into the Northern region.
In the South some States passed no law on this matter,
and in others the laws varied widely. The Alabama-
Mississippi territory act of 1815 provided for the sale of
the negroes by public auction, for cash, to the highest
bidder, the informer to have half the proceeds of the
sale, and the other half to go to the public treasury.
How this law worked will appear later on. In North
Carolina (law of 1816) one-fifth of such sales went to
the informer. In Georgia the slaves, by the act of
December 18, 1817, might be " sold, after giving sixty
days' notice in a public gazette," or " if the society for
the colonization of free persons of color . . . will
undertake to transport them to Africa . . . at the
sole expense of said society, and shall likewise pay all
expenses incurred by the State since they had been
captured and condemned, His Excellency the Governor is authorized and requested to aid in promoting
the benevolent views of said society."

No national law regulating the disposal of such
slaves as these was passed until after the war of 1812.

Another matter considered in connection with this
bill introduced on December 3, 1806, was the coastwise
traffic between the States. The efforts to prohibit that
failed ; but the law provided that no ship under forty
tons should engage in it. There was no limit to the
number of slaves that might be carried, although a
voyage from the Chesapeake to New Orleans frequently lasted as long as one from Africa to the West
Indies.

The penalties provided for the violation of this act included forfeiture of the ship "to the United States"; a fine of $20,000 to be imposed for fitting out a slaver; a fine of $5,000 for aiding in the importation of slaves; a fine of from $1,000 to $10,000, with imprisonment ranging from five to ten years, for taking slaves on board a ship from Africa or any other foreign country, and a fine of $800 for buying a smuggled slave.

Furthermore, the President was authorized to "cause any of the armed vessels of the United States" to be employed "to cruise on any part of the coast of the United States" in search of smugglers. In case any such smuggler was captured the captain, on conviction, was to be imprisoned from two to four years, and fined not to exceed $10,000. The ship was to be forfeited as a prize to the naval ship. The negroes were to be delivered to the State authorities where the slaver prize found a port.

This law has often been mentioned as the result of a great moral victory—and, of course, it did show some progress in American civilization; but when the facts are considered we find that practically it was a mere dead-letter.

CHAPTER XI

TALES OF THE EARLIER SMUGGLERS

A Slaver's Ferry Between Havana and the Florida Ports—
Amelia Island as a Smugglers' Headquarters—The Bara-
taria Pirates and the Smuggling Trade—Extent of the
Illegal Traffic—A Georgia Governor who Left His Post to
Become a Slave Smuggler.

NOTHING like a complete story of the smuggling
traffic in slaves carried on along the coasts of the
United States has ever been told, and none can be
told, because of conditions that were very well stated
by Congressman Lowndes, of South Carolina, in the
House on February 14, 1804. " With navigable rivers
running into the heart of it [his State], it was impos-
sible, with our means, to prevent our Eastern breth-
ren, who in some parts of the Union, in defiance of the
authority of the general Government, have been engaged in this trade, from introducing them into the
country. The law was completely evaded, and for the
last year or two Africans were introduced into the
country in numbers little short, I believe, of what
they would have been had the trade been a legal
one."

The fling at New England ship-owners was entirely
justified by the facts, but it will also be observed that
citizens of South Carolina were the receivers of the
goods stolen by the New England thieves.

Another popular Florida port was Pensacola. There was a regular slave-ferry between Havana and Pensacola in the days when Florida was Spanish territory. When General Jackson seized Pensacola in the spring of 1818, Colonel Brooke captured the slaver *Constitution* with eighty-four negroes on board, while Lieutenant McKeever, of the naval forces, captured the *Louisa* and the *Marino* with twenty-three slaves between them. All these slaves were destined to the United States for a market. Considering the fact that three slavers were found in or near the port at one time, it is fair to suppose that at least one slaver a week was the average of arrivals.

Congressman Mitchell estimated that 20,000 were smuggled in each year. In 1810 President Madison referred to the traffic and said he believed that "just and benevolent motives" would " be felt by Congress in devising further means of suppressing the evil."

On January 22, 1811, Secretary of the Navy Paul Hamilton wrote to Captain H. G. Campbell, the commanding naval officer at Charleston, S. C., saying: "I hear, not without great concern, that the law prohibiting the importation of slaves has been violated in frequent instances at St. Mary's (Ga.), since the gunboats have been withdrawn from that station. . . . Hasten the equipment of the gunboats . . . and despatch them to St. Mary's with orders to use all practicable diligence."

The extent of the traffic here mentioned may be imagined from what is said by the author of the " Voyage of the Ship *Two Friends*," who was in a position to learn some of the facts before he wrote his book.

"During the existence of the impolitic intercourse act
. . . so great was the trade [of all kinds] that three
hundred sail of square-rigged vessels were seen at
one time in the Spanish waters waiting for cargoes."
Amelia Island was then probably the most populous
slave-station in the world.

Another notable slave-station on the borders of the
United States previous to the war of 1812 was that
established at Barataria, southwest of New Orleans,
where Jean Lafitte ruled. Lafitte's piratical cruisers
captured many slavers and brought their cargoes to
Barataria. The bayous between that and the Mississippi were admirably suited for smugglers. They
smuggled all kinds of goods, but negroes paid best of
all. The operations became so bold that the national
Government sent Commodore D. T. Patterson, of the
navy, and Colonel George T. Ross, of the army, with
forces that destroyed the settlement. The vessels and
other property captured sold for $50,000, and this sum
was distributed among our men who had part in the
expedition. That so great a sum was realized at
forced sale for the property shows how extensive the
Barataria smuggling business was.

After the war of 1812 the people chiefly concerned
in the Barataria colony went to Galveston Island and
there established what they called the Government of
the new State of Texas. This was done in 1817 but
the exact date is not recorded. The ruling spirit was
"Commodore Louis Aury," who had held a commission in the New Grenada navy, but was in 1817 acting under a commission issued by Herrero, an agent
of the Mexican republic. Aury called himself the
Commodore of the allied fleet in the war with Spain.

He set up a court of admiralty, and before this court he brought and condemned such vessels as his "allied fleet" could capture. To dispose of the property thus obtained he adopted the smuggling tactics of the Baratarians, and he found plenty of men in New Orleans ready to assist him.

On April 5, 1817, Aury removed his establishment down to Matagorda, and thence to Amelia Island, Fla., where the smuggling operations became so bold and extensive as to attract the attention of the whole nation.

In fact the business became so profitable that Governor David B. Mitchell, of Georgia, resigned his honorable office and became the United States agent of the Creek Indians in order that he might, as he supposed, safely participate in the smuggling traffic. The Creek agency was in the midst of the wilderness then lying between the Georgia settlements and the new plantations of the Louisiana purchase. Mitchell had the slaves taken by obscure trails to his headquarters at the agency, and he intended to distribute them thence to the Louisiana plantations. He supposed that the routes to be followed, the location of the agency, and his personal influence combined would enable him to do a wholesale smuggling business in perfect safety. But he was detected, and lost money as well as his honor. The facts in this matter can be found in the "American State Papers"—Miscellaneous—Vol. II., p. 957. It seems necessary to give the authority for this story lest it seem wholly incredible.

The documents in this case (p. 962) show that "prime fellows were offered at Amelia at $250 ; ordinary from $175 to $200." Therefore the net profit in smuggling slaves into the United States varied between $350 and $500 per head.

Details of the smugglers' methods are to be had in sufficient number, but the story of one trip described by Drake may suffice for all.

"The kaffle, under charge of negro drivers, was to strike up the Escambia River, and thence cross the boundary into Georgia, where some of our wild Africans were mixed with various squads of native blacks and driven inland till sold off, singly or by couples, on the road. . . . The Spanish possessions were thriving on this inland exchange of negroes. . . . Florida was a sort of nursery for slave-breeders, and many American citizens grew rich by trafficking in Guinea negroes and smuggling them continually, in small parties, through the Southern United States. At the time I mention, the business was a lively one."

CHAPTER XII

SLAVERS DECLARED PIRATES

Fines and Imprisonment with Rewards for Informers were not Sufficient to Stop Slave Smuggling—Workings of the Prohibitive Legislation Illustrated by the Doings of the Knife-Inventor Bowie and the Pirate Lafitte—Slaves Sold by the Pound—Influences that Led to the Piracy Act.

WITH the smoke of the Amelia Island camp-fires in their eyes and nostrils our national legislators undertook the task of making the dead law of 1807–08 a live one. Both houses brought in bills, but adroit politicians were found in Congress to see that the power of the bills was weakened, if not destroyed, and in this case these politicians succeeded in ruining the bill altogether.

The bill as passed was entitled "An act in addition to 'an act to prohibit the introduction [importation] of slaves into any port or place within the jurisdiction of the United States, from and after the first day of January in the year of our Lord 1808,' and to repeal certain parts of the same." It was approved on April 20, 1818.

It might with truth have been entitled "An act to promote treachery among smugglers." Congress supposed that by appealing to the cupidity of the lawless, and offering a cash premium to those smugglers who

127

would inform on their associates, the morality of the smuggling region would be improved.

To show how the new law differed from that of 1807, it may be said that the old provided (see sec. 2) that "every such ship" engaged in importing slaves "shall be forfeited to the United States." The law of 1818 [sec. 1] provided "forfeiture, in any district in which it may be found; one-half thereof to the use of the United States, and *the other half to him or them* who shall prosecute the same to effect."

But while the act was ineffective, as a whole, one section (8) is of interest because it clearly shows a tendency in Congress at that time to extirpate the trade. Therein it was provided that in "all prosecutions under this act the defendant or defendants shall be holden to prove" that the slave " which he or they shall be charged with having brought into the United States, or with purchasing, selling, or otherwise disposing of" the same, "was brought into the United States at least five years previous to the commencement of such prosecution, or was not brought in, holden, or purchased, or otherwise disposed of contrary to the provisions of this act." To throw the burden of proof on the accused was a novelty in American legislation.

The next year Congress acknowledged this law to be inefficient by passing the act of March 3, 1819. While this was in the House of Representatives, Nelson, of Virginia, had a clause inserted providing the death penalty for engaging in the traffic. This penalty was struck out in the Senate. Du Bois notes here that Congress was already beginning to divide on party as well as geographical lines when slavery

IT WAS A MALARIA- OR DEATH-MIST THAT I SAW RISING.

See page 75.

was to be considered. The bill of 1818 was favored, he says, "by the South, the Senate, and the Democrats." The law of 1819 was the bill of the North, the House, and by the as yet undeveloped but growing Whig Party.

Under the act of 1819 the President, in section 1, was "authorized, whenever he shall deem it expedient, to cause any of the armed vessels of the United States to be employed to cruise on any of the coasts of the United States or territories thereof, *or of the coasts of Africa* or elsewhere . . . to seize" American slavers. The proceeds from the sale of seized slavers were to be divided between the nation and the naval crew, and a bounty of $25 for each slave so taken was given in addition.

The President was also authorized to appoint an agent to reside on the coast of Africa (Liberia) to receive and care for the negroes when captured.

Plain citizen informers were to have half the proceeds of fines and $50 cash bonus for each slave captured in the course of smuggling operations.

On the other hand, in the interests of the slavers, it was provided (sec. 5) that a naval officer must "bring the vessel and her cargo, for adjudication, into some port of the State or Territory to which such vessel so captured shall belong, if he can ascertain the same." This section was added on the motion of Congressman Butler, of Louisiana, who said he had " a due regard for the interests of the State that he represented." The slave-ships owned in New Orleans, for instance, were to be sent to New Orleans for adjudication. Section 4 provides also that "it shall be ascertained by verdict of a jury" whether a ship had violated the law.

To show how this law operated we may quote a passage from the life of the noted James Bowie, of New Orleans, who gave his name to the famous sheath-knife. Bowie, with his brother, Rezin Bowie, and two others of like adventurous minds, formed a company, and entered into treaty with Lafitte, who was still a chief spirit among the smugglers in the Gulf region. Lafitte "sold them sound and likely blacks off his slave-ships at the rate of a dollar a pound. That made the average price something like $140 the head. In the open market the blacks would fetch from $500 to $1,000 each." Having purchased the slaves, the ordinary course was to sneak them through bayous to any purchaser they could find. But taking advantage of the law that gave half the proceeds of the sale of the negroes to the informer, besides a bounty of $50 a head, they often informed on each other, under false names, and had the slaves condemned and sold by due process of law. At the sale no competitors appeared, because it was fully understood in the community that Bowie was evading the law, and, slaves being in demand, public sentiment supported the transaction. The Bowies made a good profit in these transactions, the Government officials got fat fees, and planters got the slaves at market prices.

"Altogether the company realized a profit of some $65,000 within a couple of years. But the business involved such mummery and flummery of false names, pretended disguises, and pretended seizures that the Bowies pretty soon tired of it." They were a rough lot, but they were not sneaks. They proved, long be-

fore the words were written, that "it is physically im-
possible for a brave man to make money the chief
object of his thoughts."

When Congress reassembled in December after passing the act of March 3, 1819, the slave-trade came up for
further consideration. The colonization society that established Liberia, of which the story is to be told, had,
by its activity in various ways, increased the public
knowledge of the evils of the slave-trade. Furthermore, it was able to reach the slave-holders for two
reasons. First, it was pledged not to interfere with
American slavery. Second, it was formed for the
specific purpose of removing the slave-holder's chief
eyesore, the free negro, out of the United States.

Undoubtedly there were in the United States many
people who were opposed to the trade because of principle. But the student cannot overlook the fact that
the feeling against the trade was able to make head-
way because there was no financial interest in slaves
or slavers at the North, outside of a few ports, and at
the South there were increasing numbers of slave-owners who had slaves to sell through the natural increase
of their holdings. The fact that the coastwise trade
had demanded consideration in the previous legislation
is significant. Virginia was already the mother of an
export trade in slaves. To prohibit absolutely the
importation of wild Africans was to " bull the market "
for the planters who found more profit in breeding
slaves than in cultivating the soil.

Meantime the privateers, so-called, of the Latin-
American republics had made alarming attacks on
our unarmed merchant ships. Pirates swarmed over
the West India seas, and their doings were justly be-

lieved to be, in many cases, chargeable to the slave-trade. The slavers turned pirates, and the pirates turned slavers, as occasion warranted.

In short, from good motives and bad, a bill was brought in that became the act of May 15, 1820. Because it provided the death penalty for participation in the slave-trade, the sections pertaining to the trade shall be given in full :

And be it further enacted, That, if any citizen of the United States, being of the crew or ship's company of any foreign ship or vessel engaged in the slave-trade, or any person whatever being of the crew or ship's company of any ship or vessel owned in whole or in part, or navigated for, or in behalf of, any citizen or citizens of the United States, shall land, from any such ship or vessel, and, on any foreign shore, seize any negro or mulatto, not held to service or labor by the laws of either of the States or Territories of the United States, with intent to make such negro or mulatto a slave, or shall decoy, or forcibly bring or carry, or shall receive, such negro or mulatto on board any such ship or vessel, with intent as aforesaid, such citizen or person shall be adjudged a pirate, and, on conviction thereof, before the Circuit Court of the United States for the district wherein he may be brought or found, shall suffer death.

And be it further enacted, That, if any citizen of the United States, being of the crew or ship's company of any foreign ship or vessel engaged in the slave-trade, or any person whatever, being of the crew or ship's company of any ship or vessel owned wholly or in part, or navigated for, or in behalf of, any citizen or citizens of the United States, shall forcibly confine, or detain, or aid or abet in forcibly confining, or detaining, on board such ship or vessel, any negro or mulatto not held to service by the laws of either of the States or Territories of the United States, with intent to make such negro or mulatto a slave, or shall, on board any such ship or vessel, offer or attempt to sell, as a slave, any negro or mulatto not held to service as aforesaid, or shall, on the high seas, or anywhere on tide-water, transfer or deliver over, to any other ship or vessel, any negro or mulatto not held to service as aforesaid, with intent to make such negro or mulatto a slave, or shall land or deliver on shore, from on board any such ship or vessel, any such negro or mulatto, with intent to make sale of, or, having previously sold, such negro or mulatto as a slave, such citizen or person shall be adjudged a pirate, and, on conviction thereof before the Circuit Court of the United States for the district wherein he shall be brought or found, shall suffer death.

An an expression of the sentiment of the nation as a whole at that time, regarding the slave-trade, that law seems unmistakable. But that was not all that Congress did to show the determination of the nation to suppress the slave-trade. On May 12th a resolution passed the House as follows :

"That the President of the United States be requested to negotiate with all the Governments where Ministers of the United States are or shall be accredited, on the means of effecting an entire and immediate abolition of the slave-trade."

The law was comprehensive and just. Though limited in life to two years, it was made perpetual by a joint resolution on January 30, 1823. This resolution looked to a wide-spread and thorough enforcement of the law. It was a good resolution.

CHAPTER XIII

INTERNATIONAL CO-OPERATION FOR SUPPRESSING THE TRADE

Work of British Diplomacy among the Continental Powers— When Spain agreed to Abolish the Slave-trade for a Money Consideration and Failed to Fulfil Her Contract— A Free Offer of " Sailors' Rights " which We Refused to Accept—A Shameful Record in American Slaver Legislation—The Ashburton Treaty.

MEANTIME in Europe, in 1804, an act in Denmark, abolishing the slave-trade, which had been passed in 1792, came into operation. In 1806 Great Britain proposed to the United States a treaty "of amity, commerce, and navigation" under which the two nations were to "agree to use their best endeavors to procure the co-operation of other Powers for the final and complete abolition of a trade so repugnant to the principles of justice and humanity," but the United States refused to join.

Finding that the act of 1807 was ineffective, the British legislators in 1811 declared participation in the trade by any British subject a felony punishable with fourteen years' transportation.

On March 29, 1815, Napoleon, on assuming control of France after his return from Elba, decreed the abolition of the slave-trade. This decree was re-enacted in 1818 by the Bourbon dynasty.

By the treaty of Ghent, concluded December 24, 1814, Great Britain and the United States agreed to "use their best endeavors" for the abolition of the trade.

On February 8, 1815, "five of the principal Powers [Great Britain, Russia, Prussia, Austria, and France] made a solemn engagement, in the face of mankind, that this traffic should be made to cease, in pursuance of which these Powers have enacted municipal laws to suppress the trade."

On July 23, 1817, Great Britain and Portugal made a treaty whereby "ships of war of each nation might visit merchant vessels of both, if suspected of having slaves on board, acquired by illicit traffic." This related only to trade north of the equator. On September 23d of the same year Spain agreed, in consideration of £400,000 paid to her as an inducement, to "the immediate abolition of the trade north of the equator, its entire abolition after [May 30] 1820, and the concession of the same mutual right of search which the treaty with Portugal had just established." Portugal agreed to abolish the trade absolutely in 1823.

Mixed courts were also established under these treaties, but it is certain that their work was nullified as far as possible by both the Spanish and the Portuguese people.

Few events more honorable to the British nation are described in history. Her willingness to pay out $2,000,000 thus early for the benefit of a down-trodden race was not only a forerunner of a similar and much greater sacrifice, but it was characteristic. That Spain should have been willing to accept pay under such circumstances, and that she should then have de-

liberately violated the contract for more than fifty
years, was also characteristic.

On May 4, 1818, Great Britain and the Netherlands
contracted for a mutual right of search.

On March 3, 1824, Great Britain enacted that any
British subject found guilty of engaging in the slave-
trade should " be deemed and adjudged guilty of
Piracy, Felony and Robbery," and should " suffer
Death without Benefit of Clergy, and Loss of Lands,
Goods and Chattels, as Pirates, Felons and Robbers
upon the Seas ought to suffer."

In 1713 the Assiento treaty was considered a mar-
vellous triumph of diplomacy. In 1824, the trade contemplated in that treaty was denominated piracy.

On November 6, 1824, Sweden and Great Britain
agreed to a mutual right of search on the slave-coast,
and England invited us to join in such an agreement,
though we declined. In 1820 she had done this also.
In 1830 Brazil prohibited the slave-trade under severe
penalties. In 1831 and 1833 Great Britain and France
agreed to a mutual right of search, and then together
invited the United States to join them under the
same agreement.

This is an important matter from one point of view.
We fought out the war of 1812 because of British ag-
gression ; but, in spite of our victories, the British,
when peace was made, refused to concede our de-
mands in regard to the searching of our ships and the
impressment of our seamen. But now, in order to
suppress the slave-trade, England not only asked for
the right of search within a definitely described space,
but in terms both renounced all claims to a right of
search elsewhere and offered to agree that no seamen

should be impressed from the ships so to be searched.
A pirate had been, by the law of nations, a man without a country : he was the lawful prize of all honest
ships. The plain meaning of any statute declaring the
slave-trade piracy was to deliver up the slaver to the
vengeance of any lawfully authorized patrolman of the
high seas. Great Britain was entirely willing that
every British slaver should be treated so, but even
John Quincy Adams was constrained to declare to the
British authorities, at the behest of the slaver power,
that the slave-trade was "statutory piracy"—something different from high-sea robbery. It could never
be allowed by the people of the United States that an
American slaver should be treated as a high-sea robber
by any other power than an American court!

Anyone wishing to examine the original documents
pertaining to this branch of the subject will find them
in Sen. Doc., 18 Cong. 2 Sess. I. No. 1 ; and American
State Papers, Foreign, V. Probably the most interesting of our public documents on the slave-trade are
No. 283, Ho. Rep., 27 Cong. 3d Sess., and Doc. No.
115, Ho. Ex. Rep. 26 Cong., 2d Sess.

The radical trouble was that cotton-growing was becoming so profitable that people who in 1808 thought
slavery a dying institution had become aggressive for
the spread of it, and so men were always found in Congress to block legislation that would hinder the slavers.
Worse yet, the law of May 15, 1820, was thwarted by
the United States District Attorneys who brought
indictments against captured slavers under previous
Statutes. It appears by the records, for instance, that
in the United States District Court for Maryland, Captain Jason L. Pendleton, of the slaver brig *Montevideo*,

was sentenced on Monday, June 23, 1845, by Justice Heath, on an indictment found under the statute of May 10, 1800.

Our act of 1819 for the suppression of the slave-trade had carried an appropriation of $100,000 for enforcing it. In 1823 we appropriated $50,000. Thereafter at wide intervals smaller appropriations were made. In 1834 only $5,000 was appropriated, and not another cent was given after that until 1842. Moreover the money given in these appropriations was not wholly for the direct suppression of the slave-trade, the bulk being devoted to the support of negroes captured from smugglers and of that ill-gotten enterprise the Liberia colony.

Nevertheless a treaty in relation to the slave-trade was yet to be made with Great Britain. The causes leading to this treaty were numerous, the chief cause being the exposures, frequently made, of the doings of American slave-ships. Our cruisers captured a slaver now and then. The *Cyane*, the first sent out, captured five, of which the *Plattsburgh* was most notorious. The tales of these slavers, and the perjury which their owners never hesitated to commit (see the slaver cases in reports of U. S. Supreme Court) were shocking.

But the feature of the trade that proved most shocking was the use of the American flag for its protection. Because we had deliberately and emphatically declared that no foreign ship should search an American merchant-man in time of peace, the slavers flocked to our flag. Slavers were captured, too, that carried blank American papers to be filled out as occasion required. The *Constitucao*, with blank papers signed by United States Consul N. P. Trist, of Havana, was one. (See Sen. Ex. Doc. 125, 26 Cong. 2 Sess.)

Then came Buxton's book on "The Slave-trade and Its Remedy." It was an appeal to sentiment rather than reason, but it gave facts which have never been seriously disputed, and which excited horror wherever read. It was proved beyond dispute that more than 250,000 lives were deliberately sacrificed in Africa and more than 60,000 on the high seas in each year in order to supply the Americans with the slaves wanted.

Meantime there were a number of matters in controversy between Great Britain and the United States, and the people were sensible enough to get commissioners to consider them instead of going to war. Out of this commission came a treaty of which the part important for this history was a solemn agreement on the part of the United States to keep a squadron of warships cruising on the African coast to operate in conjunction with a British squadron of equal force for the suppression of the slave-trade.

Our laws had, therefore, permitted the President to send naval vessels to Africa to suppress the slave-trade. By Article 8 of what is known as the Ashburton Treaty we became in honor bound to "maintain in service, on the coast of Africa, a sufficient and adequate squadron or naval force of vessels, of suitable numbers and descriptions, to carry in all not less than eighty guns, to enforce, separately and respectively, the laws, rights, and obligations of each of the two countries for the suppression of the slave-trade."

Daniel Webster signed the treaty for the United States, and Lord Ashburton for Great Britain, on August 9, 1842.

CHAPTER XIV

TALES OF THE OUTLAWED TRADE

How the Laws were Interpreted—Slavers that would Make a
Fierce Fight—Famous American Privateers that Became
Slavers—Whole Cargoes of Slaves Thrown to the Sharks
to Avoid the Confiscation of Vessels—Tales of the *Rapido,*
the *Regulo,* and Hemans's *Brillante*—A Cargo of Slaves
Bound to Anchor and Chain and Thrown Overboard—A
Slaver Who Coolly Murdered His Sweetheart and Child—
A Trade that was Lucrative in Proportion to Its Heinous-
ness.

THE trade being now outlawed, the tender solicitude
of legislators for what were called lawful traders,
that is, traders who exchanged rum and cast-iron
muskets for ivory and palm-oil, was so great that
the law regarding slavers was restricted in ridiculous fashion. Nor was it ridiculous alone from the
point of view of one who sees that to trade rotten
muskets for good palm-oil and ivory was degrading to
the trader. The lawful traders, so called, on the coast
of Africa were almost invariably panders to the slave-
traders. Says Drake, in his "Revelations of a Slave-
Smuggler" (p. 66), regarding the goods he exchanged
for slaves: "Our spirits, cotton, powder, and guns
are bought from English trading stations on the Congo.
We buy on the coast, and pay higher for these goods,
rather than that the old factories should break up ;

140

they being very convenient sometimes as temporary slave depots."

To protect these panders it was provided in the conventions between England and various continental governments for the suppression of the trade that "no *visit* or detention can take place, except by a commissioned officer having *express instructions* and authority for the same ; nor can he detain or carry into port any vessel so visited, except on the single and simple fact of slaves found on board."

In like fashion it was held for a time in our courts that the presence of slaves on a ship was necessary to secure her conviction as a slaver. Eventually the presence of slave-goods was sufficient to convict, and in English courts the slave-goods were also considered good evidence as to an English slaver, but it appears that when a slaver under any other flag was to be tried there it was always necessary to show that the slaves were on board lest some harm be done to the "lawful trader."

As to the effect of the laws on the slavers—the men in the trade—there is one feature of this effect that seems to have been overlooked by the writers who have considered the subject. It is a most interesting fact that from the moment it was outlawed the slave-trade became more attractive to certain adventurous spirits of the age. For it need not be doubted that men lived in those days whose souls as eagerly sought the thrill of a fight for life — whose souls more eagerly sought for the smell of burned gunpowder and the sight of blood-splashed decks than for the gold doubloons that rewarded the successful voyage. The sea was alive with men who had served in the privateers during the long-continued wars, and real black-flag pirates abounded. To declare by legislative enactment that the slave-trade was illegitimate was for these men but to increase its attractiveness.

Still all slavers were greedy, more or less, and an immediate effect of the laws was to reduce the price of the slaves on the coast of Africa. Slavers, when the trade was lawful, had often paid as high as $100 for a good negro in Africa. The price now went down to $15 and $20. On the other hand, the market in the West was at least made firm. Prices were not raised in Cuba or Brazil, perhaps, but there was never any trouble in disposing of the cargo even when the slaves were reduced so much that they had to be carried ashore in arms, like babes, from the landing barges. The price in the United States would have been increased by the laws, only for the fact that Virginia had become an exporter of slaves; but, as it was, the price was already high enough to yield a profit that now seems well-nigh incredible. The slave that cost $20 in Africa would, if landed in fairly good order in Georgia bring no less than $500 net, even after allowing for dividing with underground agents there. In short, outlawing the trade enhanced its attractiveness in every way to the wilder spirits.

So it came to pass that a naval cruiser's success in capturing a slaver sometimes depended on the relative size, speed, and armament of the two ships. In the House Reports No. 348, 21st Congress, first session, is a list of eighteen slavers that resisted the cruisers by force of arms. Of these, five were former well-known American privateers. They were the *Commodore Perry*, the *Commodore McDonough*, the *Argus*, the

Criterion, and the *Saucy Jack*. Built for speed, and manned by men who had seen service in voyages for legal plunder, these privateers were the ideal slavers. They went down the slave-coast flying any flag that pleased the fancy. If they fell in with a slaver of less force than their own they transferred her cargo to their own decks. If they met a small cruiser they cleared for action, and it is a matter of record that they made such a good fight, in many cases, that they beat off armed agents of the law. Of the five, four were captured, but, each of the brief reports says, "after a severe action." The *Saucy Jack* seems to have justified her name, for she not only escaped capture but " convoyed several vessels to and from the coast."

The *Paz* was a noted Yankee slaver. " Under the American flag" she "beat off the *Princess Charlotte* and killed several of her men." The *Camperdown*, an English slaver brig, of sixteen guns, "destroyed the sloops *Rambler* and *Trial*, of Sierra Leone, and carried off their black crews as slaves," and " made slaves of all the people going off in canoes."

And then there was the slaver *Velos Passagero*. She carried twenty guns and a crew of one hundred and fifty men. Having five hundred and fifty-five slaves on board, she fell in with the British sloop-of-war *Primrose*, but not until forty-six of her crew had been killed and twenty wounded by the war-ship's close-range fire, would she yield. The sloop lost three killed and twelve wounded.

Extended reports of these battles are not now to be found, but the brief statements of losses show how stubbornly the outlaws resisted arrest when they were of a force to give hope of success.

On the whole, it is likely that during the earlier years of this century nearly a fourth of all the slavers overhauled by the cruisers made some sort of resistance with arms, and as late as 1845 we have an account of the massacre of the crew of the cruiser *Wasp* on the African coast. But that one was a sorry victory for the slavers, for it led to the just order to British cruisers to give no quarter to a slaver that resisted, and resistance immediately went out of fashion.

Previous to that massacre, according to Captain Canot, British officers were known, sometimes, to admire a good fighter so much as to let him escape— even to help him escape after capture!

When there was no hope in a fight, the only way to escape condemnation was to get rid of the slaves before the cruiser could get an officer alongside. That legislators should not have foreseen the effect of this law or its interpretation, is no great wonder. But that the rule should have remained in force as it did is a shocking exhibit in the civilization of the day.

The facts as to the workings of this rule appear in the brief stories of scores of captured slavers. There was the case reported by the British cruiser *Black Joke*, Captain Ramsey, for instance, in the Bight of Benin, in 1831. Captain Ramsey sent two tenders in chase of the Spanish slaver brigs *Rapido* and *Regulo* that were seen coming, loaded with slaves, from the Bonny River in September of that year.

"When chased by the tenders both put back, made all sail up the river, and ran on shore. During the chase they were seen from our vessels to throw their slaves overboard, by twos, shackled together by the ankles, and left in this manner to sink or swim as

SHE WALKED TO THE SHIP'S SIDE AND DROPPED THE BODY INTO THE SEA.

See page 78.

they best could. Men, women, and children were seen in great numbers, struggling in the water, by everyone on board the two tenders; and, dreadful to relate, upward of one hundred and fifty of these wretched creatures perished in this way." So runs Captain Ramsey's report. Captain Ramsey said afterward that he and his men distinctly saw the sharks tearing the negroes as they struggled in the water.

In order to save the two vessels, that together were not worth $10,000, from condemnation in court, these slaver captains deliberately murdered one hundred and fifty human beings.

The *Regulo* was overhauled while she had yet two hundred and four on board out of her original cargo of four hundred and fifty. The *Rapido* had not one left on board when overhauled, but, two of her cargo having been picked up, it was possible to prove that they had been on board of her, and she was made a lawful prize.

One of the most murderous stories of captains who were anxious to get rid of their slaves is told of the slaver *Brillante*, commanded by an Englishman named Homans, who in ten voyages had landed 5,000 negroes in Cuba. She was brig rigged, carried ten guns, thirty sweeps (big oars), and a crew of sixty men in the forecastle. An English cruiser that attacked her was so badly cut up that her crew had to abandon her. When, on another occasion, the boats from a sloop-of-war attacked the *Brillante* they were driven off with great slaughter. Finally Homans found himself trapped by four cruisers that came upon him from all quarters, and there was no escaping them.

However, the wind died away and night came on

before the cruisers arrived at their range, and at that Homans set his largest anchor ready for dropping. Then he hauled the chain-cable out through the hawse-pipe and stretched it around the ship outside the rail, by means of slender stops, and to this chain he bound every slave on board—about 600 in number, piling them up at the rail and securing their arm-shackles to it by strong cords through the chain links. There the slaves remained until the war-ship boats were heard coming near at hand, and then he cast loose the anchor, and down all those slaves were carried into the sea.

Although the crews of the war-ship boats had heard the noise and the outcries when the slaves were sent to the bottom, and the hold of the slaver contained indisputable evidence that the slaves had been there but a few minutes before the boats arrived, they had to let the slaver go free. Indeed, Homans jeered in their faces and defied them as they stood on his deck, but they had no redress.

The British war-ship *Medina* on boarding a slaver off the Gallinas River found no slaves on board. The officers learned afterward, however, that her captain really had had a mulatto girl in the cabin. He kept her for some time after the cruiser appeared, but see-ing that he was to be boarded, and knowing that the presence of one slave was enough to condemn the ship, he tied her to a kedge anchor and dropped her into the sea. And so, as is believed, he drowned his own unborn flesh and blood, as well as the slave girl.

In view of the murders invariably committed on board the slavers, it is not without interest to recall that among those captured in 1828 was one on its way from Africa to Brazil, that was called the *Bom* [*Sic.*] *Jesus*.

One might multiply these stories by going to the slaver cases that reached the United States Supreme Court, but it would only add to the number of facts without increasing knowledge. The student who may wish to pursue the subject will find all the stories he needs in " Wheaton's Reports," vols. 5, 8, 9, 10, and 12; "Cranch's," 2, and 6; "Peters's," 11, 14, and 15 ; all of which were carefully examined in preparing this work.

As to the extent of the trade previous to the Ashburton treaty, we can find ample confirmation of all the estimates ever made by the abolitionists if we will examine the official reports of consuls and naval officers. Captain Trenchard of the *Cyane*, for instance, reported three hundred slavers on the coast while he was there. Over two hundred slavers were nominally owned in Havana in 1818. During the year 1828 no less than 46,160 slaves were imported into Rio de Janeiro alone, and the slavers bringing them reported deaths on the way numbering 5,592 (see *Niles's Register*, January 9, 1830). Cuba and Brazil had become the great landing territories for slaves, for it was an open traffic there in spite of solemn treaties. The trade was indeed " lucrative in proportion to its heinousness " ; the traders " to elude the laws " did but " increase its horrors."

CHAPTER XV

THE NAVY AND THE SLAVE-TRADE

Story of the Half-hearted, Wholly Futile Work of Blockading the African Coast—Reward of an Officer Who Earnestly Strove to Stop the Trade — An Interesting Period in the Career of Commodore M. C. Perry — American and British Squadrons Compared—The Sham Work of the Buchanan Administration.

THE first act of Congress to connect our navy in any way with the slave-trade was that of 1800. Section 4 provided "That it shall be lawful for any of the commissioned vessels of the United States to seize and take any vessel employed in carrying on trade, business or traffic, contrary to the true intent and meaning of this, or the said act, to which this is in addition."

Nothing to attract public attention was done by the navy under this act until 1811, when Captain H. G. Campbell, senior officer at Charleston, was ordered by Secretary Paul Hamilton to "hasten" to the St. Mary's River as already noted, to stop the smuggling trade. A similar use of the navy was made in the trouble with Aury.

After the act of March 3, 1819, several ships were sent to the coast of Africa. The *Cyane*, Captain Ed-

ward Trenchard, twenty-four guns, sailed from the
United States in January, 1820 ; the corvette *Hornet*,
Captain George C. Reed, eighteen guns, sailed in
June, 1820, and the corvette *John Adams*, Captain
H. S. Wadsworth, twenty-four guns, sailed July 18,
1820. To these was added the schooner *Alligator*,
Captain R. F. Stockton, that sailed on April 3, 1821,
reached the coast on May 6, started home in July,
sailed out once more on October 4, and left for home
on December 17, thus making two cruises on the coast
in that year. The schooner *Shark*, Captain M. C.
Perry (a brother of the hero of Lake Erie), sailed on
August 7, 1821, and was on the slave-coast a part of
September, all of October, and a part of November.
Trenchard of the *Cyane* reported that there were three
hundred slave-ships on the coast. Perry reported, "I
could not *even hear* of an American slaving vessel ;
and I am fully impressed with the belief that there is
not one at present afloat." *

The *Cyane* captured five American slavers, the *Hornet* took one, the *Alligator* took four, but three of
these were recaptured from the prize-crews. The
fourth, the *Jeune Eugene*, reached Boston and was
condemned.

In 1822, Captain R. T. Spence succeeded Trenchard in
command of the *Cyane*. The Secretary of the Navy,
Samuel L. Southard, in his report dated December 1,
1823, says that both Spence and Perry "have, for
short periods, cruised on the coast of Africa to carry
into effect the intentions of the Government. . . .
[they] neither saw nor heard of any vessel, under the
American flag, engaged in the slave-trade."

* " American State Papers—Naval Affairs," Vol. I., p. 1099.

Thereafter the work of the navy in suppressing the slave-trade was confined to "occasional visits" to Liberia until 1839, when the shame aroused by the frequent reports of the use of the American flag by slavers caused some activity. The brig *Dolphin*, Commander Bell, and the schooner *Grampus*, Lieutenant Paine, were sent to the coast, where they merely scared a few slavers. Captain John S. Paine, of the schooner *Grampus*, having been ordered to the coast of Africa to suppress the slave-trade, assumed that he was to do everything possible within the laws of nations to accomplish the work. He found many slavers provided with double sets of papers. Now, under the laws he could do nothing with slavers bearing any flag but his own. But England having made treaties including the right of search on that coast with a number of continental powers, her cruisers were able to search almost any ship visiting the coast except those under the American flag.

To meet the scheme of double papers Captain Paine and Commander William Tucker, of the British forces, agreed that whenever the *Grampus* fell in with a vessel manifestly a slaver, and showing any flag except the American, she was to be detained (but not searched) until a British cruiser could be brought to search her. On the other hand, every slaver showing the American flag was to be detained (but not searched) until the *Grampus* could come to make the search. When Paine reported his plan to Washington he was promptly told that his plan was "contrary to the well-known principles" of his Government. The slave-coast was 3,000 miles long. Paine was ordered to "suppress" all American slavers there with the *Grampus*.

In 1842 came the Ashburton treaty, under which we were bound to keep on the coast of Africa a "*sufficient* and *adequate*" squadron or naval force of vessels for the "*suppression*" of the slave-trade. England was bound by the same words.*

The fact is, we never had *on the coast*, for any length of time worth mention, even the eighty guns which the

* A message of President Buchanan under date of April 21, 1858, to the Senate of the United States contains the following tables showing how each nation kept its faith:

The following is a statement of the number of vessels and total number of guns of the British squadron on the west coast of Africa on the 1st of January of each year from 1843 to 1857, inclusive:

Year.	Vessels.	Guns.	Year.	Vessels.	Guns.
1843........	14	141	1851.......	26	201
1844........	14	117	1852.......	25	174
1845........	20	180	1853.......	19	117
1846	23	245	1854.......	18	108
1847........	21	205	1855.......	12	71
1848	21	208	1856.......	13	72
1849	23	155	1857.......	16	84
1850........	24	154			

The following is a statement of the number of vessels and total number of guns of the United States squadron on the coast of Africa on the 1st of January of each year from 1843 to 1857, inclusive:

Year.	Vessels.	Guns.	Year.	Vessels.	Guns,
1843........	2	30	1851.......	6	96
1844........	4	82	1852.......	5	76
1845........	5	98	1853.......	7	136
1846........	6	82	1854.......	4	88
1847........	4	80	1855.......	3	82
1848........	5	66	1856.......	3	46
1849........	5	72	1857.......	3	46
1850........	5	76			

treaty called for. The table shows how many guns were on ships *assigned to the squadron*, not what were actually on the coast.

Commodore M. C. Perry was the first officer to command on the coast under this treaty. He got his orders on April 6, 1843, and reached Liberia on August 1st. It was almost a year after the treaty was ratified before we had a gun on the coast, and even then she was at an American free colony.

Perry's ship was the *Saratoga*, a frigate, whereas light, swift schooners were needed. However, the *Porpoise* did cruise on the slave-coast. The instructions to her commander, as issued by Perry, may be summed up in the following paragraph taken from a letter under date of August 1st:

It is only necessary for me to add that under no circumstances are you to permit, without resistance *to the extent of your means*, any foreign vessel of war, of whatever *force* or *nation*, in the exercise of any assumed *right* of *search* or visitation, to board in your presence (you having first forbidden it) any vessel having the American flag displayed. But you are to use every vigilance in examining, with your own officers, the vessels so displaying the American flag, and if it shall be found that she has unauthorizedly hoisted such flag, you will, if there be no cause for detention by yourself, immediately give notice to any vessel of war in sight that she (the vessel examined by you) has no rightful claim to your interference or protection.

The *Decatur* also cruised on the slave-coast. Her orders said :

It is my desire that you show your ship at as many of the slave and trading marts as time and circumstances will authorize.

This order calls to mind a certain game constable
employed by the State of New York to prevent poach-
ers from killing deer in the Adirondacks out of season.
Some law-abiding citizens having notified him that
Utica scoundrels were killing deer by jacklight on Little Black Creek Lake, the constable said :   " I'll stop
them at once." Thereat he drove as near to the lake
as the woods roads would permit, and stuck his card in
the splinters of a dozen or more stumps along the
route.

"There," said he ; "that 'll scare 'em out." Then
he drove home again.

Having fallen in with a British cruiser, Perry got
authentic stories of two American vessels, the *Illinois*
and *Shakspeare*, that brought slave-goods to the
coast, and, after discharging, were loaded with slaves.
Then the American flag was hauled down and away
they went over the sea. The *Illinois* hailed from
Gloucester, Mass., and was the property of Pason &
Co.

In the instructions issued to British naval officers
on the coast after the treaty of August 9, 1842, appears the following sentence :

"The commanding officers of Her Majesty's vessels
on the African station are to bear in mind that it is
no part of their duty to capture or visit, or in any
way interfere with, vessels of the United States, whether these vessels shall have slaves on board or not."

The British officers had only to satisfy themselves
that a ship really had American papers. They were
even instructed to manœuvre so as to board without
bringing to the vessels flying the American flag.

Meantime it should be noted that Perry had been

instructed that it was "highly desirable that a vessel of each nation should, as far as possible, cruise in company with a vessel of the other, so that each may be in a position to *assert the rights* and prevent the abuse of the flag of its own country."

"To assert the rights" was put first, of course; joint cruising was desirable rather to keep the British from American traders than to suppress the slave-trade.

"*Joint* cruising" was one of the stock terms in use at Washington before the civil war. Every administration believed in "joint cruising" as the right way to suppress the slave-trade.

Says the chaplain to the African squadron in the years 1855–57, himself a believer in slavery, in his book "Adventures and Observations on the West Coast of Africa" (p. 318): "The joint cruising has been from the first in spirit and letter dead. It is hardly worth while to inquire upon which party the greater blame rests in the non-fulfilment of this provision; but it is certainly true that the object of the treaty could be better carried out by a hearty and well-understood co-operation. The prevailing indifference on this subject may be seen by the following statement: The flagships of the American and British squadrons on the coast in the years 1855, 1856 and part of 1857 met but once, and that at sea. They were two miles apart; they recognized each other by signal, and by the same means held the following communication:

" ' Anything to communicate ? '

"Answer.—' Nothing to communicate.' "

Perry himself summed up the result of his work as

the commander of the American squadron for the suppression of the slave-trade on the coast of Africa in a letter to Secretary A. P. Upshur, dated September 5, 1843 :

"I cannot hear of any American vessels being engaged in the transportation of slaves ; *nor do I believe there has been one so engaged for several years.*"

He deliberately ignored the cases of the *Illinois* and the *Shakspeare.* Moreover that was in 1843, when a condition of affairs prevailed at Rio Janeiro that led the United States Consul, a Wise of Virginia, to write, a little later : "We are a byword among nations—the only people who can fetch and carry any and every thing for the slave-trade without fear of the English cruisers"—a condition wherein the slavers were allowed "to pervert our glorious flag into the *pirate's flag.*"

We can now see how it happened that Perry was honored with the command of the Gulf squadron in the war with Mexico, and with the command of the Japan expedition in later years. The name of Oliver Hazard Perry will be held in honor while glorious deeds afloat are remembered ; the name of his brother Matthew C. Perry brings the flush of shame to the face of everyone who is proud of the navy's glory. The system of patrol was utterly wretched and Perry was a fit man for commodore under such a system.

After Commodore Perry the next naval officer in interest to this history was Admiral Andrew Hull Foote, in those days a lieutenant-commander, who was sent to the coast as captain of the brig *Perry.*

Foote was a sincere man, but, being of a sanguine temperament, he was mistaken as to what was really accomplished by the American squadron. He carried out the spirit of his orders, and so devoted very much more time to hunting for British cruisers that were accused of boarding American ships than to suppressing the slave-trade. In a book that he wrote about his experience on the coast, he devotes more space to telling how " the American commodore argued from documents and other testimony that *bona fide* American vessels had been interfered with, and, whether engaged in legal or illegal trade, they were in no sense amenable to British cruisers" than to the capture of slavers.

Nevertheless Foote did good work on the coast, and his book has some good stories of slaver days in it. Among the best of the stories is that of the capture of the American bark *Pons*, Captain James Berry, on November 30, 1845. The *Pons* had been at Kabenda for twenty days during which the British cruiser *Cygnet* remained on blockade. But a time came when the *Cygnet* had to leave for supplies. At that Captain Berry turned the ship over to one Gallano, a Portuguese slaver, and at eight o'clock that night the *Pons* was under way with nine hundred and three slaves under her hatches.

To avoid the cruisers off shore the *Pons* kept alongshore during the night. At daylight, seeing the upper sails of a British cruiser out at sea, she furled her own sails and drifted so close in to the breakers that the natives came to the beach expecting her to come ashore. However, she neither grounded nor attracted the British cruiser, and eventually she stood out to sea.

As it happened, the *Yorktown*, Captain Bell, was lying in her path, but the slavers supposed she

THEN HE CAST LOOSE THE ANCHOR.

See page 146.

was a British cruiser and at once set the American flag. That settled her fate, for she was a legitimate prize to an American warship. The Portuguese captain put on his hatches, but no sooner had the American naval officer boarded her than they were taken off and the "slaves gave a shout that could have been heard a mile."

A remarkable fact about this ship was that she had no slave-deck. About eight hundred and fifty of her cargo had been stowed in bulk on the water-casks and provision barrels in the hold. Eighteen had died during the night. In the fourteen days that elapsed while going to Monrovia one hundred and fifty more died, and eight died while in the harbor before they could be landed.

Foote's chief prize was a big ship called the *Martha*. The *Perry* arrived at Ambriz on June 5, 1850, in search of her flagship, *John Adams*, but learned that she had gone to Loanda. Sailing thence the *Perry*, while at sea, next day, saw a big ship standing in for the coast and at four o'clock in the afternoon brought her to. At this time the *Perry* had not shown her flag and the stranger hoisted the American flag. Her name and port, "*Martha*, New York," were painted across her stern.

Accordingly a boat was sent to her, when her captain saw, by the uniform of the boat's officer, that the *Perry* was an American cruiser. At that the *Martha's* American flag was hauled down and the Brazilian hoisted, while a writing-desk was thrown overboard on the side of the *Martha* opposite the boat.

A Portuguese who claimed that he was captain protested when Lieutenant Rush, the American boarding officer, reached the deck, but Rush said that the ship had made herself a legal prize as a pirate by throwing away her papers. The writing-desk had been picked up and its contents discovered meantime. The American captain, though disguised as a common sailor, was identified. He finally admitted that she was a slaver and that she was to have taken on board 1,800 slaves that night.

The *Martha* and all her crew were sent to New York, where the ship was condemned. Her captain was released on $3,000 bail, which he at once forfeited. The mate was not well taken care of by the slavers, for he was sent to prison for two years.

The farce which our courts played regularly in those days was exhibited in this case, for the percentage payable to the slaver captain on an ordinary cargo of slaves landed—say four hundred—was $12,000. Rarely, if ever, was a greater bail than $5,000 exacted.

And it is to be further noted that when Foote captured the *Martha* he had "her crew put in irons," but "both American and Brazilian captains, together with three or four cabin passengers [probably slave-agents] were given to understand that they would be similarly served in case of the slightest evidence of insubordination!" *They* lived in the cabin.

Foote declares that the yellow fever, that has carried off its tens of thousands of white men, was generated from dead slaves in the slavers at Rio de Janeiro in 1849. He is right beyond question. It is a fact that may even now give us pause. The sufferings of the slaves were avenged on the white race with merciless sev.erity. There *is* a universal law of compensation.

Foote believed that the activity of the American squadron in the early fifties had broken up the slave-trade. How far wrong he was appears in the report of the Secretary of the Navy for 1860, wherein no less than eleven slavers are mentioned as prizes taken in 1859. The one most important to this history was the ship *Erie*, captured on August 8, 1860, off the Congo, by the sloop-of-war *Mohican*, Commander Sylvester W. Godon. She had eight hundred and ninety-seven slaves on board. She landed those that survived at Monrovia.

The number of slavers captured that year was most remarkable. At first glance one would say that the Buchanan administration was honestly striving to enforce the law, but the fact is, this flurry of activity was but a part of a scheme to enlarge the borders of American slave territory. Buchanan and his Secretary of the Navy, Isaac Toucey, deliberately told Congress that the administration was "active in its endeavors to suppress the African coast slave-trade," when they were active only in an effort to annex Cuba to the United States. On the same page where Toucey boasts that his department was "active" (p. 9, report of the Secretary of the Navy, 1860), he says:

"Cuba is now the only mart in the world open to this trade. . . . *If Cuba were to pass under the Constitution of the United States by annexation* the trade would then be effectually suppressed."

CHAPTER XVI

FREE-NEGRO COLONIES AND THE SLAVE-TRADE

England Led the Way by Establishing a Colony at Sierra Leone
to Provide a Home for Negroes Carried from the United
States during the Revolutionary War — The Enterprise
Saved by the Sturdy Maroons—Origin of the American
Society for Colonizing Free People of Color—Life of the
Colonists at Cape Mesurado—The Nation of Liberia Or-
ganized—An Ape of Philanthropy.

WHEN Lord Mansfield declared on June 22, 1772,
that the negro Somerset must be set free a new question arose for the consideration of the ruling race. It
was a question of growing importance, as time went
on, and it was eventually transferred to America,
where it became, at last, for a time, the most serious
subject of discussion before the people of the United
States: What shall be done with the freed man?

It was easy to provide for Somerset and all those
who were liberated, one at a time, under Lord Mansfield's order, but after our Revolutionary war the
English had a larger share in the problem, because
of the number of American slaves they had carried
away during that war.

Most of the slaves thus taken had been landed
in Nova Scotia, where there were no slaves. The
negroes would have been more comfortable in the

West India islands, but thither they could not be taken because the slave-owners were beginning to see that free negroes were a serious disturbing element among the plantations. It rarely occurred to a negro slave that he was born to any rights equal with those of his master, until he saw free negroes work or not at pleasure, and receive wages when they did work. Then he began to think. It was a serious matter for the owner when the slave began to think. It became most serious in Jamiaca when the slaves fled to the mountains for freedom and there organized communities that were naturally predatory—so serious, indeed, that troops were sent into the mountains to hunt out with bloodhounds these maroons, as they were called. The troops settled the question there temporarily by killing many of them and capturing more.

Meantime the British people found the ports of England swarming with negroes discharged from the navy at the end of the war. So three classes of free negroes were to be considered at the end of the eighteenth century—the slaves from America, the sailors from the navy, and the Jamaica maroons.

As a first step in solving the problem an Englishman named Smeatham, of London, who had lived for a time at the foot of the Sierra Leone Mountains, conceived the idea of forming an African colony with these freedmen. The subject appears to have been broached first in 1783; it is mentioned in Sharp's "Memoranda" on August 1st of that year, and Sharp adopted the idea. Eventually the Government granted an allowance of £12 per head for the expense of transportation ; a ship was chartered ; a sloop-of-

11

war—the *Nautilus*, Captain Thompson—was sent as
convoy, and on April 8, 1787, away they sailed for
Sierra Leone. There were more than four hundred
ex-slaves gathered in English ports, and sixty Euro-
peans in the party. Reaching the coast they purchased of a native chief, known as King Tom, the Sierra
Leone colony site, and the African colonization scheme
was inaugurated.

How the first colonists died by the score from ma-
larial fever; how the Nova Scotia negroes were
brought there to die in like fashion ; how drunkenness
and indolence helped on the anarchy ; how a war with
the natives nearly wiped out the remnants of the settlement, and how, at last, in 1800, a band of maroons
from Jamaica, five hundred and fifty strong, came and
saved the adventure from utter failure—all that is too
long a story to be told here. We need only remember
that the men who saved the colony were those who
had been too proud to remain slaves, and had found
liberty in the wilds of the Jamaica mountains until
hunted down by bloodhounds set on by the Christian
hosts of the king.

When the colony of Sierra Leone had been established as a refuge for freed negroes the story was told
in the United States, where the slave-owners were ever
in fear of a servile insurrection led by free negroes.

Here, then, was the solution of the most troublesome
question known to slave communities ! It appealed to
the humanitarian who was willing to sacrifice his
property in slaves whenever he could do so without
violating the laws of his State, as well as to the slave-
owner whose brutal tyranny was the result of innate
cowardice. The one was glad of a chance to give free-

dom to his slaves; the other was glad to get rid of the free negroes, whom he hated because he feared them.

Still another class heard of the plan with joy—the indolent philanthropists, who would do something for unfortunate people if it did not involve too much trouble.

Looking the matter squarely in the face, a century after the plan was inaugurated, we can see unmistakably that the African freedmen colony scheme was founded chiefly on indolence and cowardice. If we speak of Liberia alone we must say it was founded on cowardice and indolence. At the same time many upright, sincere, self-sacrificing people were connected with both colonies. The tales of what some people suffered to promote the interests of the unfortunate blacks are heart-rending.

It is true that the idea of forming a free-negro colony was considered in the American colonies before our Revolutionary war, but it was not until Sierra Leone was established that anything practical was done here. On December 31, 1800, the Virginia House of Delegates requested the Governor to correspond with the President "on the subject of purchasing lands without the limits of this State whither persons *obnoxious* to the laws or *dangerous* to the peace of society may be removed." (Italics not in original.) Other State Legislatures considered the matter in similar fashion. There was talk of sending the free negroes to Hayti. A part of the Louisiana Territory was considered as a possible location. Finally, on December 21, 1816, a meeting was called in Washington "for the purpose of forming a colonization society." Henry Clay presided, and on the 28th the organization of the society was completed. The constitution adopted began as follows:

ART. 1. This society shall be called "The American Society for Colonizing the Free People of Color of the United States."

ART. 2. The object to which its attention is to be exclusively directed is to promote and execute a plan for colonizing (with their consent) the free people of color, residing in our country, in Africa, or such other place as Congress shall deem most expedient. And the society shall act, to effect this object, in co-operation with the general Government, and such of the States as may adopt regulations upon the subject.

The constitution was written by Robert Wright, of Maryland. Elias B. Caldwell, Clerk of the United States Supreme Court, was the chief orator of the occasion, but John Randolph also spoke. Mr. Justice Bushrod Washington was elected President. Henry Clay and Andrew Jackson were among the seventeen Vice-Presidents, of whom, by the way, only five were from the free States. It is asserted that all of the twelve managers were slave-owners, and certainly nearly all were so, while Bushrod Washington was engaged in the domestic slave-trade when not hearing cases on the bench.

J. H. B. Latrobe, in an address delivered before the society on January 20, 1880, describes the organization and the motives of the original members accurately. He said that some "regarded it as a missionary enterprise only." Others "hoped that it would lead to a separation of the negroes from what the masters said was *an injurious contact with their slaves.*" Others "believed that it would tend to raise the negroes of the United States to civil and religious liberty in the land of their forefathers. Others again supported it as likely to promote emancipation. Others looked forward to the commerce that would follow the establishment of a colony on the borders of a vast continent . . . and others again fancied that, in some undefined way, African colonization would afford a solution of the negro question in this country."

That is to say, those who "sincerely desired to afford the free black an asylum from the oppression they suffered here, and by their means to extend to Africa the blessings of Christianity and civilization"; those who wished to accelerate emancipation; those who expected to enhance the value of slaves by getting rid of the meddlesome free blacks; those who wanted to promote trade in ivory and palm-oil, and the half-hearted philanthropists who sought "relief from a bad population *without the trouble and expense of improving it*," all these were united in an organization for colonizing our free negroes in Africa. At their meetings "the devoted missionary, ready to pour out his life on the sands of Africa," was "jostled by the trafficker in human flesh," and the "humble, self-denying Christian listened to the praises of the society from the unblushing profligate." Mr. Latrobe, speaking to and for the society, says "*it was well that all this was so. Co-operation, regardless of motive*, was the necessity of the occasion."

Congress by the act of March 3, 1819, authorized the President to employ naval ships "to cruise on any of the coasts of the United States or territories thereof, or of the coasts of Africa or elsewhere," to capture slave-ships; and, further, "to appoint a proper person or persons, residing upon the coast of

Africa, as agent or agents for receiving the negroes, mulattoes, or persons of color, delivered from on board vessels seized in the prosecution of the slave-trade by commanders of the United States' armed vessels."

The Rev. Samuel Bacon, on the society's recommendation, was appointed both Government and colonial agent. Mr. John P. Bankson and Dr. Samuel A. Crozer, agents of the society, were associated with him. The ship *Elizabeth* was chartered by the United States (Congress had appropriated $100,000) and eighty-six colored emigrants were picked up and carried to Boston. These agreed, "in consideration of their passage and other aid," to " prepare suitable accommodations for such Africans as might be rescued from the slave-ships by American cruisers."

On February 6, 1820, the *Elizabeth* sailed. A landing was made at Sherboro, where a New Bedford negro named Kizel had established a colony of eight families at his own expense. Then "fever made its appearance among the people, who were loud in their complaints," * and with very good reason, too, because twenty-five of them died of it, and Bacon himself fell a victim. The remaining emigrants went to Sierra Leone, and colonization was in a bad way.

But meantime the warship *Cyane* and others had sent several slavers loaded with wild negroes to the United States for adjudication, and to get rid of those negroes further efforts were made to establish an African colony. The Government sent the war schooner *Alligator*, Captain R. F. Stockton, to explore the African coast, and Captain Stockton selected Cape

* Foote's Africa and the American Flag, p. 113, line 18.

Mesurado as a suitable location, on December 12, 1822.

When an attempt to get the land by treaties with the natives was made the chiefs foresaw that the colony would interfere with their profitable slave-trade, but Stockton's diplomacy prevailed, and a tract, including Cape Mesurado, that lay between the Mesurado and Junk rivers, " thirty-six miles along the sea-shore with a breadth of two miles" was secured.

To this site Dr. Ayres carried the remaining colonists who had gone to Sierra Leone, landing them on a small island "amidst the menaces of the natives." Then, by an arrangement with a neighboring chief, they crossed the river to the north and "erected a number of comparatively comfortable buildings."

Meantime many colonists had been attacked with the unavoidable fever, and while this was spreading they had a fight with the natives. An English crew on a captured slaver let her drive ashore. The natives came to loot her and the colonists helped the English, with loss of life on both sides. They saved the vessel but incurred the hatred of the natives. The truth is the scheme would have failed then and there but for the courage and fortitude of Elijah Johnson, one of the colored men.

When Dr. Ayres, the white agent, and a number of the emigrants returned to Sierra Leone, "almost in despair" (as the society's records say, but wholly in despair, probably), Johnson said:

"I have been two years searching for a home and I have found it, and I shall stay." And he did stay. Neither the Pilgrim fathers nor the followers of Lord Baltimore nor the French Huguenots had worse troubles to face than he, nor did any one of them all show a manlier front.

Not to follow all the distressful details of the founding of the colony, it may be said that the inevitable fever was their chief enemy, even though at one time they had to fight so many natives that the balls from their nine-pounder cannon literally passed through so many bodies as to spend their entire force in that fashion.

Until 1824, the colonists were, on the whole, acting in self-defence. In 1824, no less than fifteen slavers were loading, under the guns, almost, of the colony, and there was a contract between one slave-trader and a native chief by which eight hundred slaves were to be delivered within four months. Thereat the colonists assumed the offensive, attacked the chief who had made this contract, destroyed the slave-pen, released the slaves, and compelled the chief to sign an agreement to abandon the trade.

Following this a slaver settlement called Tradetown, where there were three slave factories and two armed slave-ships, was attacked. The fighting lasted from April 10th to April 12th, inclusive (1824), the settlement was captured, and "the explosion of two hundred kegs of powder consummated the destruction of Tradetown."

"The annihilation of Tradetown and of the slave factories was a severe blow to the traffic, which was felt as far south as the Bight of Benin," says Commodore Foote.

This much was done by free colored men. In view of that fact the reader will find the following extracts from publications of the Colonization Society remarkable reading. Said Henry Clay in a speech found in the *African Repository*, Vol. VI., p. 12:

" Of all the descriptions of our population the free persons of color are by far, as a class, the most corrupt, depraved, and abandoned." The same periodical, Vol. VII., p. 230, called them "an anomalous race of beings, the most depraved upon earth." An editorial Vol. I., p. 68, said : "There is a class among us, introduced by violence, notoriously ignorant, degraded and miserable, *mentally diseased, brokenspirited.*"

Meantime the colony had been named Liberia by the home society, from the Latin word *liber*, a free man.

In 1834 the Maryland Colonization Society, formed on the same lines as the original association, sent out an expedition on the brig *Ann*. She called at Monrovia, got twenty-five acclimated citizens, and, going down to Cape Palmas, formed an independent colony, landing on February 11th. "A very valuable tract of land at Bassa Cove was purchased for the Young Men's Colonization Society of Pennsylvania," this year, and the ship *Ninus* landed one hundred and twenty-six emigrants there, of which one hundred and ten were "slaves, freed by the will of Dr. Hawes, of Virginia." Meantime the original colony was widening its borders.

Then came (in 1836) Thomas Buchanan, a colored man, agent of the New York and Pennsylvania societies to Monrovia. He was a born leader. He saw the evil likely to arise through trade jealousies between the separate and independent though neighboring colonies, and a union of all was effected under a constitution providing for a government somewhat like that of the United States. No white man could become a land-owner under the laws, but all adult black males were voters, and slavery was absolutely prohibited. It failed of making a nation of the colonies only because "the American Colonization Society retained the right to veto the acts of the local legislature."

This was an anomalous condition of affairs, but it served very well until Buchanan, as governor of the united colonies, began levying duties on goods imported at old-established trading posts lying within the territory over which his people had obtained control. There were factories for legitimate trade that had been in existence longer than the Liberian settlements. The traders having made the establishments by the same sort of contract that existed between the natives and the Liberians, believed themselves to have as good rights to free trade there as the Liberians had. Buchanan acted on the theory that the Liberian Government had the same control over its territory as our Government has over the United States.

As a matter of fact Liberia had then no standing as a government. It consisted merely of a lot of settlements controlled by a society of private American citizens. So when Buchanan seized by force the property of certain British citizens he went too far. The British Government naturally protected its citizens, and the *John Seyes*, a colonial schooner, was taken by way of reprisal.

This led to an appeal to the American Government. It was proposed that the United States adopt the colony as Great Britain had adopted Sierra Leone; but we would have no entangling over-sea alliances, and so missed a chance to get a foothold on what is now a continent well worth exploiting. So a compromise was effected with the British.

After a time Buchanan died in the harness and Joseph J. Roberts succeeded him as Governor. He was a statesman as well as a natural leader. He had been trained under the masterful Buchanan, and the region under his control continued to flourish, after a fashion, until the evil of its anomalous position among nations compelled an organization as a republic. Accordingly a convention was called, a Declaration of Independence was proclaimed, a new constitution written and adopted, and on August 24, 1847, the lone-star flag of the Republic of Liberia was flung to the breeze.

A census report published in the *African Repository* for 1847 (p. 192) shows that in 1845 the immigrant population amounted "to nearly 5,000," to which was added a native population of which "estimates vary from 10,000 to 15,000. Of these about 300 are so far civilized" that they were permitted to vote at elections. In this report the startling statement is made that of all the emigrants from the United States to Liberia no less than one-fifth had died of the so-called acclimatizing fevers! The average life of a white man there, as learned on another authority, was three years.

Ten years later (1857) the Rev. Charles W. Thomas, the naval chaplain already quoted, reported Liberia as having a coast line of "over 600 miles, embracing a country of 30,000 square miles, and a population of over 10,000 civilized blacks and 200,000 natives" (uncivilized). This may be considered a friendly estimate.

In 1857 the Government income was $47,556 ; disbursements, $47,048. Said Thomas : "There is a surplus in the treasury of $500 ; but truth demands the statement that many of the Government officials, noble and patriotic men, have deferred drawing the full amount of their salaries, small as these are, until the country is more able to pay them."

Of the history of Liberia since that time little need be said. Perhaps as a last item the fact that it stood, hat in hand, before Congress in 1879, begging for the pitiful sum of $25,000, will suffice.

The old society has still life enough to support a secretary and publish an annual report, but its power for creating discontent among the American negroes is well-nigh ended. It was an ape of philanthropy from the day of its organization, and the industrial schools for colored men that are flourishing at the end of the nineteenth century will soon strangle—or starve—it to death, when its memory will be found worth preserving only as a warning.

THEY WERE SEEN TO THROW SLAVES OVERBOARD SHACKLED TOGETHER.

See page 144.

CHAPTER XVII

TALES OF THE COASTWISE SLAVE-SHIPS

Colored Men from New York Prison Sent to New Orleans and
Sold—Stealing Slaves in New Jersey for the Southwest
Market—Coastwise Slavers that Lost their Human Car-
goes in British Islands—Madison Washington a Negro
Worthy of his Name—Joshua R. Giddings and the Coast-
wise Trade—Extent of the Coastwise Traffic.

WHEN the United States prohibited the slave-trade
by the act of March 2, 1807, a reservation was carefully made in favor of the coastwise trade of the nation itself. Sections 8 and 9 provided that no "ship
or vessel of less burthen than forty tons," in the coast
trade, should take on board or transport any slave "to
any port or place whatsoever" under penalty of $800
for each slave. Any "ship or vessel of the burthen of
forty tons or more . . . sailing coastwise from
any port in the United States to any port or place
within the jurisdiction of the same," might carry
slaves, however, on making out "duplicate manifests
of every such negro," with a full description of each,
and delivering "such manifests to the collector of the
port," before sailing. There was absolutely no limit
specified as to the number to be carried, nor was there
any provision for the safety, let alone the health and
comfort, of the slaves so to be carried. And that, too,

in the face of the fact that a voyage from the breeding plantations in Virginia to the market in New Orleans might, and often did, last as many days as the shorter voyages from Africa to the West Indies.

Curious tales are told regarding the working of this law. The first, so far as found by the writer hereof, is in an incidental reference in a public document quoted in *Niles's Register* for September 30, 1815, wherein is mentioned the fact that "a young woman named Catharine Richardson" was "in the schooner *Cynthia*, of New York, Charles Johnson, master." Johnson having touched at a British port, his slave managed to get ashore and found friends who secured her freedom under the British law that prohibited the importation of slaves. That occurred in 1811.

A New Orleans paper quoted in the *Register* for February 8, 1817, said:

"Some inhuman speculator at New York has disburthened the prison of that city of seventy or eighty negroes, by procuring their imprisonment to be commuted for transportation, and shipping them for this place—where they arrived a few days ago. But he has been disappointed of his profit, and we doubt if he will clear even the freight of his cargo. The corporation has very properly ordered the vessel containing this gang of thieves and ruffians to proceed without the limits of the city."

In that day newspapers did not employ professional humorists, but the editors wrote humor unintentionally and in spite of indignation. Fancy sending seventy able-bodied negroes beyond the limits of New Orleans, in 1817, as a means of depriving the holder of a profitable sale! If the editor had added that conscienceless New York was forcing an odious traffic upon helpless but indignant Louisiana as the wicked British forced the odious traffic on their helpless but indignant American colonies the editorial would have been worth printing as a red-ink broadside to be framed for lasting preservation.

A similar editorial item in June, 1818, says that "negro trading seems to be actively carried on through certain great villains holding their headquarters in New Jersey, from whence, we trust, the good people of that State will soon chase them. A vessel with thirty-six persons of color has been seized at New Orleans for not having a manifest, etc., as required by law. She received her cargo of human beings near Perth Amboy. It is probable that the greater part of these unfortunate creatures were stolen."

That is to say, free negroes in New Jersey were kidnapped, taken on board ship, and carried to New Orleans for sale—an exact counterpart of one feature of the prohibited African slave-trade. Mr. Niles did not give the name of the vessel, but it was the brig *Mary Ann*, and she sailed from Perth Amboy on March 10, 1818.

Near the end of 1829 the schooner *Lafayette* sailed from Norfolk for New Orleans, having on board a cargo of more than one hundred slaves. The slaves rose against the crew, but were subdued, and twenty-five of them were "bolted down on the deck" for the remainder of the voyage. That was the first "mutiny" in the coastwise trade that I have found. Others more interesting followed.

To appreciate fully the following stories the reader

must recall an act passed by the British Parliament
in 1833, to take effect August 1, 1834. This act was,
in one respect, the most notable in the history of human liberty, for while in a thousand other cases men
have done noble deeds for their own liberty, in this
one the British nation voluntarily taxed itself to the
extent of £20,000,000 to provide liberty for an inferior
race. During more than thirty years Great Britain
spent regularly more than £500,000 a year on her African squadron and gave the lives of many of its best
sailors for the benefit of the despised negro, and meantime, at one appropriation, added £20,000,000 to all
that expense. As a national recognition of the obliga-
tion which the dominant race *owes* to all inferior races
the work of Great Britain in connection with negro
slavery and the slave-trade remains unequalled in the
history of the world.

On August 1, 1834, slavery for life was forever abolished in the British nation. The legislation of all
other nations of that day was based on the inhuman
idea that mental and physical superiority in one race
gave it the right to deprive inferior human beings of
liberty and to extort from them labor for the aggran-
dizement of the superior race.

In the year 1830 the city of Alexandria, Va., was
what may be called the Omaha of the human cattle
trade. Slaves were gathered there by traders for transfer to the ever-craving maw of the Gulf States. In
the course of the year the brig *Comet* was loaded there
with slaves and cleared for New Orleans, but on the
way she was wrecked on the False Keys of the Bahama
group. Wreckers carried crew and slaves to Nassau,
where the authorities held that the slaves were free,

because, as alleged, the British laws prohibited the introduction of slaves.

The brig *Encomium*, from Charleston for New Orleans, with slaves, met the same fate in the same locality, with the same result to the slaves, early in 1834.

The *Enterprise*, with a cargo of slaves from the District of Columbia—Washington was noted for its slave barracoons in those days—also carrying slaves for the New Orleans market, was compelled by stress of weather to put into Bermuda on February 20, 1835.

The "Friendly Society" of colored people of the town at once got out writs of *habeas corpus*, served them upon the people interested, and had all the negroes, seventy-eight in number, brought before the proper court, with their alleged owners and the master of the ship. It was nine o'clock at night when they appeared before the court. The master of the ship had striven to have the hearing put off until next day, hoping, no doubt, to go to sea, but the effort was vain. He had also promised to give the slaves considerable sums of money if they would tell the Court that they preferred to continue the voyage.

Having all the slaves in court, the Chief Justice took his seat, called up one of the negro men, and said :

" Your name is George Hammett ; you came in the brig *Enterprise* as a slave, and it is my duty (understanding that you were kept on board that vessel against your will) to inform you that in this country you are free—free as any white person ; and should it be your wish to remain here, instead of proceeding to the port whither you was bound, to be sold or held to service as a slave, you will be protected by the authorities here ; and if you do decide to remain, you

will become, as I have observed, a free person, and will
be punished for any breach or break of the laws of this
colony ; while if you conduct yourself with propriety,
soberness, honesty, and industry, you will meet with
encouragement from the whole community. Do you
therefore wish to remain and be a free person, or continue your voyage to the vessel's destined port and remain a slave ? "

All of the slaves save a woman with five children
declared they would remain. This one family went on
to their destination as slaves.

The expressive phrase of " twisting the lion's tail "
had not been invented in those days, but twisting the
lion's tail was much more common then than even in
those recent years before our war with Spain had
shown us what a real and natural bond of sympathy
existed between the two English-speaking nations.
And the manner in which members of Congress turned
and twisted the lion's tail in connection with these
slave-ship deliveries was memorable.

As to the British, their attitude was admirably portrayed by the picture of the true griffin in Ruskin's
" Modern Painters."   They were at once reposeful and
alert, and withal ready to fulfil national obligations.

International law, which is presumably founded on
natural rights, demanded that all the property on
those vessels should be held sacred for the owners, but
straightway there arose a question as to the property
right of masters in their slaves. Under the laws of the
United States that right was granted [See the fugitive
slave laws]. Under the laws of Great Britain that
right had been everywhere abolished within her jurisdiction on August 1, 1834.

After the matter had been fully discussed, Lord Palmerston said that the slaves taken from the *Encomium* and the *Comet* had been unlawfully freed because when they came within British jurisdiction British law recognized property in human beings. Therefore they would be paid for. Those of the *Enterprise* arrived when British soil and water were free, and would not be paid for. This decision was made in 1837. From that year property in man, as a feature of international law, " ceased and determined for ever."

Nevertheless, the question was to come up again. On October 25, 1841, the *Creole*, under the command of Captain Robert Ensor, sailed from Richmond, Va., bound for New Orleans, having on board three white men as passengers, with the wife and child and a niece of the captain. In the hold were one hundred and thirty-five slaves for the New Orleans market. Two days later the *Creole* cleared the Capes and thereafter had a prosperous voyage until Sunday evening, November 7, 1841, when she was within about twelve hours' sail of Nassau.

Among the slaves was a man named Madison Washington, who was of unusual character. He had fled from slavery in Virginia some time before that, and by the underground railway had safely reached the free soil of Canada. But when there he remembered his wife away back on the old plantation, and out of love for her had returned to carry her to freedom also. He reached the plantation in safety, but before he could get away with the wife he was caught by the planter.

In those days the fate of these runaways was settled in advance. They were whipped unmercifully and then sold for the New Orleans market. To the ordinary negro, to be placed on a New Orleans ship was to end hope. To Madison Washington it brought opportunity for freedom.

At eight o'clock on the night of November 7th the crew hove to the *Creole* for the night, because of the dangers of navigation ahead of them. At 9.30 o'clock it was reported to the mate Z. C. Gifford, who had the deck, that one of the negro men was among the female slaves. At that Gifford made an examination and found Madison Washington there. Having a very wrong idea of the negro's intentions in going there, Gifford expressed his surprise, and then, having brought him on deck, was about to secure him for punishment, when Washington suddenly resisted, a shot was fired by an unknown hand, the mate was severely wounded in the back of the head, and Washington cried out:

"Come on, my boys! We have commenced and must go through with it."

He had planned a mutiny, and the other negroes were awaiting his detection in the hold as a signal for the assault on the crew.

In the fight one white man was killed and several were wounded. No negro was hurt, and in ten minutes Washington controlled the ship. Then by threats and promises he got her navigated into Nassau harbor, where she arrived on Tuesday morning, the 9th, at eight o'clock.

Of course the American consul, as in duty bound, at once made every effort to get the brig again under the command of her crew, with the slaves on board. The populace, including the authorities, knowing all about the case of the *Enterprise* at Bermuda, were

determined that the negroes should go free, and free
they became, though nineteen of them, who were
identified as active in the assault on the crew, were
taken in custody on the charges of mutiny and murder preferred by the consul and the crew. But they
were not replaced on the *Creole*.

To state the case of the slave-owners, we may quote
the words of Henry Clay when he said that the *Creole*
was carried to Nassau by "an act of mutiny and murder," and if the British authorities sanctioned "the
enormity," "Americans would be virtually denied the
benefits of the coastwise trade of their own country,
because their vessels could not proceed in safety from
one port to another *with slaves on board*." It is apparent that under the laws of the United States, as
they then stood, Mr. Clay was entirely justified in
what he said. But by the laws of Great Britain there
was no such thing as property in man. "All men
were born free," by her law, and the negroes who
were held in slavery, contrary to their will, were justified in taking the lives of their masters in order to
obtain their natural right. Having carried the brig
into British waters, the slaves, under British laws,
became free; and the result was that they all remained free except five who voluntarily continued the
voyage to New Orleans.

It is perhaps worth mentioning here that Joshua R.
Giddings, a member of the House from Ohio, prepared
a number of resolutions on the subject in which he
sustained the natural right of the negroes to liberty
and to use force to obtain it. These resolutions he
took to the House, introduced them, and gave notice
that he would call them up for consideration. For

this he was censured by the House by a vote of one hundred and twenty-five to sixty-nine. Remarkable as it seems now, the pro-slavery members were so far fanatical in their pursuit of Mr. Giddings that they refused to allow him to defend himself or even explain his object in introducing the resolutions. Such unjust action eventually did more harm to the perpetrators than to anyone else — it did harm, in fact, to no one else. Giddings resigned, went home, and was returned by his constituents within five weeks.

Thus the mutiny on the *Creole*, a coasting slaver, became one of the most important episodes in the "irrepressible conflict" that was rising between the slave and the free-soil States.

The number of slaves that were shipped in coastwise traders is now really a matter of conjecture, but one may get an idea from kindred facts. Thus the *Virginia Times*, in an article quoted in *Niles's Register* for October 8, 1836, boasts that no less than 40,000 slaves had been sold for export from Virginia to other States during the fiscal year preceding, and that the sales had brought into the State an average of $600 per head, or $24,000,000 all told. A letter to the *Journal of Commerce*, of New York, at about that period estimates the number driven (*i.e.*, sent South on foot) out of the State in a year at 20,000. This would leave 20,000 to be sent by ship.

Another estimate may be drawn from the fact that the number of slaves in the *Lafayette*, *Encomium*, *Enterprise*, and *Creole* was near one hundred per vessel. Very likely that was an average coaster cargo. Now one Alexandria firm advertised two ships a month, and there was at least, on the average, a vessel a week from that port the year round. Norfolk was a port about as lively, and Baltimore and Richmond were not far behind. Apparently two hundred vessels carried a hundred slaves each to a Southern market every year from the waters of Virginia.

In the *Democratic Review*, of New York, for July, 1858, in an article entitled "Visitation and Search of Vessels," wherein an argument is made in favor of reopening the over-sea slave-trade, the editor says of the over-sea and the coast trades :

"We aver that if one is wrong, then both are wrong ; *that if one is right, then both are right.* We enter protest against such absurd definitions and distinctions as have been made by Congress."

CHAPTER XVIII

STORY OF THE AMISTAD

A Cuban Coastwise Slaver that may have been Used to Smuggle Slaves into the United States—On the Way from Havana to Puerto Principe the Slaves Overpowered the Crew, and Started Back to Africa, but were Beguiled to Long Island—Judicially Decided that Slaves Unlawfully Held have a Right to Take Human Life in a Stroke for Liberty.

ON August 26, 1839, the United States brig *Washington*, Captain Thomas R. Gedney, was engaged in surveying the water between Gardiner's Island and Montauk Point, L. I., when a schooner was seen at anchor well in shore near Culloden Point. There were a number of people on the beach with carts and horses, and a boat was passing to and fro between the stranger and the shore.

Apparently here was a smuggler at work in broad daylight, and Captain Gedney at once sent a boat, with six armed men, in charge of Lieutenant Richard W. Meade and Passed Midshipman David D. Porter to investigate. They found her "a Baltimore-built vessel of matchless model for speed, about one hundred and twenty tons burden, and about six years old. On her deck were grouped, amid various goods and arms, the remnant of her Ethiope crew, some decked in the most fantastic manner in the silks and finery pil-

184

fered from the cargo, while others in a state of nudity, emaciated to mere skeletons, lay coiled on the decks.

"Over the decks were scattered, in the most wanton and disorderly profusion, raisins, vermicelli, bread, rice, silk, and cotton goods. In the cabin and hold were the marks of the same wasteful destruction.

"Her cargo appeared to consist of silks, crepes, calicoes, fancy goods of various descriptions, glass and hardware, bridles, saddles, holsters, pictures, looking-glasses, books, fruits, olives, olive-oil, and other things too numerous to mention." So runs an old newspaper account.

As soon as the United States officers reached her deck two white men came to them, one begging for protection, while the other, an elderly man, threw his arms around Lieutenant Meade and held him in an embrace that made the lieutenant think the man intended violence. Drawing a pistol, Meade thrust it in his face, when the man retreated, and his companion, a young man of good address, who spoke English fluently, began an explanation.

He said his name was Jose Ruiz and that of the demonstrative elder was Pedro Montez. No offence was intended by Montez; on the contrary, his embrace was but a manifestation of gratitude. The queer little schooner, he continued, was the *Amistad*, of Havana, where she was owned and commanded by Captain Ramon Ferrar. She had sailed from Havana on June 27th, bound for Guanaja, in the Cuban state of Puerto Principe, but on the night of June 30th the slaves on the ship had mutinied, killed the captain and cook, sent the two sailors ashore in the boat, and ordered him (Ruiz) and Pedro Montez to navigate the ship to

Africa. Under fear of death the *Amistad* had been steered toward the east by day, but at night she had been headed for the United States. So it had happened that they had been for several days within a few miles of Long Island, and had finally anchored where found in order to get food and water.

As to the negroes, Ruiz said that one called Antonio was the property of the slain captain, three belonged to Pedro Montez, while the remainder, forty-nine in number, were his own property.

On hearing that, Meade sent Porter ashore with four men to round up the blacks there. The blacks on shore got into their boat and started rowing out to the schooner, but Porter stopped them with a pistol shot, and took them on board the schooner under guard. Once there, their leader, called Cinque, leaped overboard with a belt containing three hundred doubloons, and went "diving and swimming like a fish" for shore, but he was hauled back on board with a boat-hook in the hands of a grinning quartermaster.

Meantime Captain Gedney had brought the *Washington* alongside, and on hearing the reports of his officers decided to take the schooner to New London, where he libelled her for salvage. And then the trouble began.

Señor A. Calderon, who was then the Spanish Minister at Washington, at once demanded the vessel and cargo under the treaty with Spain dated 1795. One article of this treaty was quoted as exactly covering the case. It said:

"All ships and *merchandise of what nature soever, which shall be rescued out of the hands of any pirates* or robbers on the high seas shall be brought into some port of either State and shall be delivered to the custody of the officers of that port, in order *to be taken care of and restored entire* to the true proprietor as soon as due and sufficient proof shall be made concerning the property thereof."

The words in italics were so emphasized when quoted in Señor Calderon's demand. Very naturally the Washington officials were entirely willing to grant the demand. Under our laws slaves were property, and here were negroes in charge of a ship which they had taken by force from its owner. Further than that, these negroes were, according to the papers of the ship and the passports of the two Spaniards Ruiz and Montez, slaves. Ruiz, for instance, produced a passport issued by the captain of the port of Havana, in due form, dated 26 de junio (June) de 1839, which read in Spanish thus: "Concedo licencia, á cuarenta y nueva negros ladinos, nombrados," etc. The names of the negroes followed.

The Spanish words are given because of their bearing on the case, as will appear further on. So far as the papers appeared, everything was in proper form.

Meantime, however, the negroes, who were put in jail at New London, had found friends who were willing to spend money to see that they had a fair trial, were that possible in the existing state of civilization. These friends saw the passport which Ruiz exhibited as proof of ownership of the forty-nine negroes, and they were able to translate it. The translation offered by Ruiz and accepted by our Government, and so printed in a message of the President on the subject, read as follows:

"I concede license to forty-nine *sound* negroes," *la-*

dinos being rendered as *sound*. As a matter of fact, *ladinos* was a local term used in Cuban law to designate slaves born in the country or imported previous to 1820. The translation was a fraud, and the beginning of a shameful attempt to deceive the people of the United States, including the courts. For it was at once learned that neither the forty-nine negroes claimed by Ruiz nor the three claimed by Montez were *ladinos*. Cuban slave-dealers had imported them from Africa in a Portuguese vessel called *Teçora*, on June 12th—fifteen days only before they were taken on board the *Amistad*. They had been landed near Havana, and taken to a barracoon near the city, and there, on June 22d, Ruiz and Montez had purchased them. The purchasers had then obtained the usual permit for taking *ladinos* coastwise. But how it had happened that the Havana official was willing to issue a *ladino* permit, when these negroes had been landed contrary to the Spanish law, does not appear in the printed proceedings.

In short, the abolitionists said these negroes, that had been taken from their African homes and carried to Cuba, contrary to the laws of Spain, were not slaves but freemen, and when they were confined as slaves on the *Amistad* they had the natural right to rise against those who restrained them, and to regain liberty even if they had to kill two men to do it.

So issue was joined, and in the course of time (1841) the case reached the United States Supreme Court, where Justice Story delivered the opinion of the court. He said that in order to sustain the claims of Ruiz and Montez " it is essential to establish : 1st. That these negroes under all the circumstances fall within the description of merchandise in the sense of the treaty. 2d. That there has been a rescue of them on the high seas out of the hands of the pirates and robbers, which, in the present case, can only be by showing that they themselves are pirates and robbers. 3d. That Ruiz and Montez, the asserted proprietors, are the true proprietors, and have established their title by competent proof."*

As to the first point, if the negroes had been lawfully held as slaves under the Spanish law, said the Justice, "we see no reason why they may not justly be deemed, within the intent of the treaty, to be included under the denomination of merchandise. . . . But admitting this, it is clear, in our opinion . . . it is plain beyond controversy, if we examine the evidence, they never were the lawful slaves of Ruiz or Montez, or of any other Spanish subject. . . . If, then, these negroes are not slaves . . . there is no pretence to say they are pirates or robbers. But it is argued on behalf of the United States that the ship and cargo and negroes were duly documented as belonging to Spanish subjects, and this court has no right to look behind these documents. . . . To this argument we can in nowise assent. . . . The very language of the ninth article of the treaty of 1795 requires the proprietor to make due and sufficient proof of his property. And how can that proof be deemed either due or sufficient which is but a connected and stained tissue of fraud? Upon the whole, our opinion is . . . that the said negroes be declared free, and be dismissed from the custody of the court, and go without date."

* Peters's U. S. Reports, vol. 15, p. 592.

The narrative of events has been interrupted in order to give the exact status of these negroes under our laws of that date, because we are thus enabled to appreciate better the attitude of the Government officials toward this case. The Spanish Minister, Calderon, claimed them not only as slaves but as murderers, and asserted that if the leaders were executed for crime in Cuba the effect would be more salutary than if they were convicted and executed in Connecticut. Our Government officials were anxious to sustain this view. United States District Attorney William S. Holabird, of Connecticut, was so anxious in the matter that he wrote to Secretary of State Forsyth to ask whether there were no treaty stipulations under which the negroes might be given up "before our court sits."

There were none, but Secretary Forsyth instructed him to " take care that no proceedings of your Circuit Court, or any other judicial tribunal, place the vessel, cargo, or slaves beyond the control of the Federal Executive." Attorney-General Grundy wrote an opinion saying he could not see any "legal principle" that would justify the Government in questioning " the papers clearing the vessel from one Spanish port to another." He added that as the negroes were charged with violating Spanish law they ought to be delivered over to Spanish courts for trial in order that the guilty "might not escape punishment." The President, he thought, ought to order the vessel, cargo, and negroes delivered to the Spanish Minister at once without any investigation.

President Van Buren did not go so far as that, but Captain Gedney was ordered to hold his vessel in readiness to go to Cuba with the negroes, and for the purpose of giving testimony " in any proceedings that may be ordered by the authorities of Cuba in the matter." This was done before the court in Connecticut had assembled to consider the case. Worse yet, the Cabinet, in anticipation that the District Court would decide against the liberty of the negroes, prepared to hurry them off to Cuba before an appeal could be taken. The proof of this is found in a letter written by Secretary Forsyth in which he said : "I have to state, by direction of the President, that if the decision of the court is such as is anticipated, the order of the President is to be carried into execution unless an appeal shall actually have been interposed. You are not to take it for granted that it will be interposed."

Had the Court decided as Van Buren hoped it would do, the negroes would have been marched from the court-room to the United States ship *Washington*, and sent, as fast as wind and tide could drive her, to Havana.

By the decision of the Court the negroes freed were only those that had been imported from Africa in the Portuguese ship *Teçora*. Antonio, claimed as the property of Captain Ferrar, of the *Amistad*, was by law a slave, and he would have been delivered to the Spanish authorities had not some conductors on the underground railroad come to his aid. He had simply disappeared. The schooner was sold for salvage. Mills' Register (October 31, 1840) says she was old and Cuban built. She sold for $245.

Drake in his "Revelations of a Slave-Smuggler" speaks of the *Amistad* as a schooner that belonged to a joint-stock slave-smuggling company "connected with leading American and Spanish mercantile houses," that used "one of the Bay Islands, so called, near the coast of Honduras," as a station where slaves were landed after the voyage from Africa. They were there restored to health and taught plantation work before being sent to market.

It is not unlikely that the energy shown by the Washington authorities in their efforts to return these free negroes to Cuba was due in part to pressure brought by New York merchants of prominence.

But the case of the *Amistad* by no means came to an end with the comprehensive decision of the Supreme Court. The Spanish authorities appealed to Congress for indemnity in behalf of Ruiz and Montez. Our executive branch of the Government was entirely willing to grant this appeal, and on April 10, 1844, Congressman Charles J. Ingersoll, of the House Committee on Foreign Affairs, brought in a report in which the committee "entirely concur with the President's intimation" that "in conformity with every principle of law and justice" the United States ought to pay for the *Amistad* negroes. It was asserted by them that "to set the slaves free cardinal principles were violated"; and that "in defiance of the law of treaties, of the law of all civilized nations and of primary principles of universal jurisprudence, were these much-abused foreigners stripped of their property ; and the pirates who, by revolt, murder, and robbery, had deprived them of it, set free."

By an examination of the documents (including House Reports No. 426, 28th Congress, 1st Session) it appears that Ingersoll in making this report deliberately falsified dates, and built his argument on a false date.

THE SLAVES ON THE SHIP HAD MUTINIED

See page 185.

The desired appropriation was not made, but as late as February 2, 1858, the claim was before Congress with a recommendation from President Buchanan that it be paid. But it never was paid, and it might now be forgotten but for the fact that the Supreme Court of the United States, when it heard the case, decided then, for the first time, that black men carried from their homes in Africa as slaves had the right, when seeking their liberty, to kill any who would deprive them of it.

CHAPTER XIX

LATTER-DAY SLAVE SMUGGLERS

Notable Slave-ships that Plied between the African Coast and
the United States just before the Civil War—When the
Wanderer Carried the Flag of the New York Yacht Club
to the Congo—Troubles of a Smuggler as described in his
Letter-book—A Movement for Legally Reopening the
Slave-trade—Dream of a Slave Empire.

THE most remarkable evidence regarding the smuggling of slaves into the United States in the decade
before the civil war is found in a series of letters
copied from the letter-book of Charles A. L. Lamar,
a citizen of Savannah and a member of a family of
high social position. These letters were rescued from
a paper mill by an unnamed writer and printed in the
North American Review for November, 1886.

The first letter referring to the slave-trade was
dated on October 31, 1857, and was written to Lamar's
father. It says:

"You need give yourself no uneasiness about the
Africans and the Slave-trade. I was astonished at
some of the remarks in your letter; they show that
you have been imbued with something more than the
'panic' by your associations North and with Mrs. ——.

For example, you say ' An expedition to the moon
would have been equally sensible, and no more contrary to the laws of Providence. May God forgive
you for all your attempts to violate His will and His
laws.' Following out the same train of thought,
where would it land the whole Southern community?

" You need not reproach yourself for not interposing
with a stronger power than argument and persuasion
to prevent the expedition. There was nothing you or
the Government could have done to prevent it. Let
all the sin be on me. I am willing to assume it all."

A letter of an earlier date (July 27, 1857) tells something more about this expedition, and also gives a
very good insight into the way President Buchanan's
administration got on with the slave smugglers. The
letter was written to Howell Cobb, Secretary of the
Treasury. It says :

" I am loath to trouble you again, but your damned
sap-head of a collector refuses to do anything. . . .
He detained my vessel eight days after she was ready
for sea, and after she had applied for her clearance
papers. Mr. Boston said she was not ' seized,' but
merely 'detained.' He said the department would
respond to any demand I might make for damages,
etc. The District Attorney and all the lawyers to
whom he applied for advice told him that there was
nothing to cause suspicion to attach to the vessel."

A bill for damages follows : " Eight days' detention
at $150 per day, $1,200 ; wharfage, etc., $120 ; total,
$1,320." It is not unlikely that the bill was paid.
Then comes this frank statement :

" I did not, in my other communication, disclaim
any intention of embarking in the Slave-trade, nor did

I say anything to warrant you in supposing I was not engaged in it. I simply declared that there was nothing on board except what was on the manifest, and that I insist there was nothing suspicious on it. I will now say, as the vessel is 1,000 miles from here, that she was as unfit for a voyage to import negroes as any vessel in port. . . . What she may hereafter do is another matter. . . . John Boston had her detained because he says he knew she would be engaged in the trade, and had heard that from men who confessed that they were eavesdroppers, who hung around my windows to listen to all conversations that took place. . . . I am coming on to bore you in person unless you will yield to my short epistles."

That to an officer who had sworn he would execute the laws!

We find in a letter of November 7th, of the same year, to N. C. Trowbridge, of New Orleans, that the venture went awry. The letter reads :

"I am truly glad to find that Grant [the slave captain] is at least honest. He has acted badly and sacrificed our interest most shamefully. His clearance papers would have taken him anywhere he wanted to go, unmolested. . . . He knew the vessel was fitted for nothing else but *the trade*, and ought to have known we would want to send her back. . . . Why did he not go to the Coast? He knew before he undertook the command that there were armed vessels on the Coast, and a number of them. He ought to have known that *he was running no risk*—that the captain and crew are always discharged. The captain of the *Albert Devereux* was here the other day. The British cruisers even let him take his gold. If Grant had been equal to the emergency we would all have been easy in money matters."

A letter of December 23, 1857, to Theodore Johnson, of New Orleans, says: "In reference to Grant, discharge him, pay him nothing, and hope with me that he will speedily land in hell."

Much talk of Lamar's financial straits follows, and then we learn the name of the vessel. "Something ought to be done *at once* with the *Rawlins*," he says.

A letter dated three days later invites L. Viana, of 158 Pearl Street, New York, to join in the slave-smuggling business, and then we learn that "Captain William Ross Postell . . . a Gent, reliable in every way, and a thorough sailor and navigator," was secured to take command of the *E. A. Rawlins*. An era of prosperity came to the smugglers, it seems, for the letters show that, in addition to the *Rawlins*, the *Richard Cobden* and the notorious yacht *Wanderer* were put into the trade. Lamar even contemplated buying a steamer. Here is what he wrote about the steamer on May 24, 1858, to "Thomas Barrett, Esq., Augusta," italics as in the original:

I have in contemplation, if I can raise the necessary amount of money, the fitting out of an expedition to go to the coast of Africa for a cargo of African apprentices *to be bound for the term of their natural lives,* and would like your co-operation. No subscription will be received for a less amount than $5,000. The amount to be raised is $300,000. I will take $20,000 of the stock and go myself. I propose to purchase the " Vigo," an iron screw steamer of 1,750 tons, now in Liverpool for sale at £30,000 cash. She cost £75,000. G. B. Lamar can give you a description of her. . . . She is as good as new, save her boilers, and they can be used for several months. If I can buy her I will put six Paixhan guns on deck and man her with as good men as can be found in the South. The fighting men will all be stockholders and gentlemen some of whom are known to you, if not personally, by reputation. My estimate runs thus :

Steamer $150,000 ; repairs, guns, small arms,
    coal, etc., $50,000...................... $200,000
Supplies, $25,000 ; money for purchase of
    cargo, $75,000........................ 100,000
                                                          $300,000

I have, as you know, a vessel now afloat, but it is, in my mind, extremely doubtful whether she gets in safely, as she had to wait on the Coast until her cargo could be collected. If she ever gets clear of the Coast, they can't catch her. She ought to be due in from ten to thirty days. I have another now ready to sail which has orders to order a cargo of 1,000 or 1,200 to be in readiness the 1st of September, but to be kept, if necessary, until the 1st of October—which I intend for the steamer—so that no delay may occur. With her I can make the voyage there and back, including all detentions, bad weather, if I encounter it, etc., in ninety days, certain and sure ; and the negroes can be sold as fast as landed at $650 per head. I can contract for them " to arrive " at that figure, *cash.* The "Vigo" can bring 2,000 with ease and comfort, and I apprehend no difficulty or risk, save shipwreck, and that you can insure against. I can get one of the first lieutenants in the navy to go out in command, and we can whip anything if attacked, that is on that station, either English or American. But I would not propose to fight ; for the "Vigo" can steam eleven knots, which would put us out of the way of any of the cruisers.

In an estimate of the steamer's profits sent to William Roundtree, of Nashville, Tenn., Lamar placed the cost at $300,000, and the income—"1,200 negroes at $650, $780,000, which leaves net profit and steamer on hand, $480,000."

In some way this scheme fell down; probably he could not raise the capital. But it is worth telling, as showing the drift of affairs in our slave territory at that time.

As to his proposal to introduce Africans as apprentices for life, to evade the letter of the law, he said in a letter to Secretary Cobb, in 1858: "I would land the cargo on the levee in New Orleans and test the legality of the matter in the courts of the United States." And because Cobb refused to sanction such a plan, Lamar asked sternly in another letter, "Has Northern public opinion, then, acquired the force of law?"

The yacht *Wanderer*, of which Lamar makes mention, was without doubt the most notable slave-smuggler known to the trade, and her story is therefore well worth giving here.

According to the records of the New York Yacht Club, the *Wanderer* was built by James G. Baylis, at Port Jefferson, L. I., for Mr. J. D. Johnson, a wealthy member of the club. She was launched in June, 1857. Her dimensions were: Length over all, 104 feet; keel, 95; beam, 26.5; depth of hold, 10.5; draught, 10.5. Her mainmast was 84 feet long and its topmast 35. The main boom was 65 feet long, and its gaff and the main gaff 35. The bowsprit was 23 feet outboard.

Captain Thomas Hawkins superintended her while on the blocks, and "to hear him tell it," said one of his friends to me, "you'd think she could fly instead of sailing." He added: "She was, however, a very fast schooner." A beautiful painting of the *Wanderer* hangs in the Yacht Club's reception room at this writing (1900).

Mr. Johnson sold the schooner to Captain W. C.

Corrie, who was elected a member of the New York Yacht Club on May 29, 1858, and he sailed for the South with her at once. Under the rules of the club Corrie was captain of the yacht. Her sailing master was a brother of the late Admiral Semmes, of the Confederate navy. Captain Corrie took her to Charleston, and there cleared out for Trinidad, as if on a pleasure voyage, although, as a matter of fact, she had a slaver outfit in her hold. Captain Egbert Farnham, a man of an adventurous career—he had been a famous overland rider in his time, and, it is said, one of Walker's Nicaragua filibusters—went along as supercargo.

From Trinidad the *Wanderer* went to St. Helena, and thence to the Congo River. She was still flying the American flag and that of the New York Yacht Club, of course, and when the British war-ship *Medusa* was found cruising for slavers on the Congo coast, Captain Corrie ran alongside and remained with her several days (according to the newspapers), during which he entertained the British officers with the best he had, and was in turn entertained in royal fashion on the war-ship. Places of interest ashore were visited in company. There was a race with a British yacht off the coast, in which, of course, the *Wanderer* won handsomely.

Farnham told the reporters, after his return, that on one occasion, after the wine had mellowed the British officers sufficiently, they were invited to inspect the *Wanderer* to see whether she was not a slaver, whereat the whole party laughed joyously. The idea that such a magnificent floating palace as the *Wanderer* was to be used as a slaver did seem extremely ridiculous to

THE HUMAN CARGO WAS UNDER THE CHARGE OF THE OLD RICE-FIELD NEGROES.

See page 202.

tion. . . . I don't calculate to get a new dollar for an old one. All these men must be *bribed.* I must be paid for my time, trouble, and advances. . . . Six of those who were left at Mont's, who were sick, died yesterday. I think the whole of them now sick will die. They are too enfeebled to administer medicine to. I am paying fifty cents a day each for all those I took up the country. It was the best I could do. . . . I tell you hell is to pay. I don't think they will discharge the men, but turn them over for trial.

Nor were his troubles solely with the Government officials. In a letter to Theodore Johnson, of New Orleans, he says that some of the planters with whom the negroes were left for safe keeping were proving recreant to the trust. He says :

I am astonished at what Governor Phiniz has written me. . . . The idea of a man's taking negroes to keep at fifty cents a head per day, and then refusing to give them up when demanded, simply because the law does not recognize them as property, is worse than stealing.

A letter from Lamar to " C. C. Cook, Esq., Blakely, Georgia," is of interest here, though I am not able to say definitely that it refers to the *Wanderer,* for Lamar had two other slavers afloat. The italics are in the original :

You are aware that it is a risky business. *I lost two out of three.* To be sure, at first knew nothing of the business. I have learned something since, and I hope I can put my information to some account. I have been in for "grandeur," and been fighting for a principle. Now I am in for the dollars.

Meantime arrests had been made. Captain Corrie was taken in custody on January 22, 1859. The date of Lamar's arrest is not recorded, as far as I can learn.

From a letter addressed to "Captain N. D. Brown," who was apparently one of the men under arrest, it appears that while in trouble himself, Lamar still stood by some of his crew, for he says :

Your attorneys will visit you before the trial. If a true bill be found against you by the grand jury, it will be done upon the evidence of Club and Harris, and of course they will testify to the same thing. In that case I think you all ought to *leave*, and I will make arrangements for you to do so, if you agree with me. I have offered Club and Harris $5,000 not to testify; but the Government is also trying to buy them. . . . I am afraid they will convict me, but my case is only seven years and a fine. If I find they are likely to do so, I shall go to Cuba until I make some compromise with the Government.

The distribution of the negroes was accomplished in the meantime. Captain Frazier, of the river-steamer *Augusta*, testified that he carried one hundred and seventy-two of the negroes from Jekyl Island to a plantation lying two miles below Augusta. It is likely that the ball mentioned by Captain McGhee was given when this cargo was taken up the river past Savannah to Augusta.

Meantime the news had created a deal of excitement in every part of the country. Congress took up the matter. On motion of Senator Henry Wilson the Senate called on President Buchanan for all the facts that the Government had. The document containing the President's reply is a leaflet. He said: "I concur with the Attorney-General [J. S. Black] in the opinion that it would be incompatible with the public interest at this time to communicate the correspondence with the officers of the Government at Savannah, or the instructions which they have received." He added a promise to "make every practicable effort" to discover "all the guilty parties and to bring them to justice."

As usual, the smugglers escaped, and the *Wanderer* was condemned. She was sold at auction, and was bid in by her former owners at a fourth of her value as a merchant schooner.

Captain McGhee, already quoted in telling of the final results of the voyage, said that the "slaves that had been purchased for a few beads and bandanna handkerchiefs were sold in the market for from $600 to $700 apiece. The owners of the vessel paid Captain Semmes $3,500 for his services and cleared upward of $10,000 apiece on the venture for themselves.

Lamar's letters do not quite agree with this so far as he was concerned personally. "I have been badly swindled," he says, "by getting into the hands of rascals and vagabonds. I am out of pocket on the *Wanderer*—had to assume all the responsibility, pay all the money, and do all the work."

It is fair to presume that he actually got back more dollars than he put in, but considered that he had lost his time—had been inadequately paid for it.

On July 21, 1859, Lamar wrote to his friend Trowbridge, at New Orleans, saying, "The *Wanderer* is going to China, and may return with coolies. They are worth from $340 to $350 each in Cuba, and cost but $12 and their passage." It is likely she did not go on this voyage. McGhee said, at any rate, that "In the spring of 1859 the *Wanderer* again sailed for the west coast of Africa, and again Captain Semmes found King Dahominey ready to trade on the most liberal terms. On the second occasion he had to go further up the river to secure the cargo, but he succeeded in delivering six hundred captives at the mouth of the river. They were more intelligent than the first cargo, lighter in color, and better in many respects than those captured nearer the coast. A number of them died during the voyage, and the *Wanderer* was put to her best speed on several occasions to get away from undesirable acquaintances, but she was never overhauled, and she arrived off the Georgia coast in December. She was caught in a violent gale, and in attempting to enter Jekyl Creek, between Jekyl and Cumberland Islands, she ran aground one stormy night, and a number of the captives escaped from the hold and jumped into the sea and were drowned. . . . The negroes were sent to New Orleans and sold, except a few that were scattered about among the Georgia planters. The profits were quite as large as from the first expedition, and but for the breaking out of the war and the blockading of the port at Savannah, the *Wanderer* might have made another voyage in 1860. As it was, she was hemmed up in the river by the blockade and finally sold to the Confederate Government."

Lamar wrote a letter regarding this second voyage that is interesting as showing the kind of a heart he had. He said :

The man who went on her before would like to go again, but he made an extraordinary claim the last time, and it, of course, was not settled in full—and he might take some advantage and *throw* us, to pay off any feeling he might have against the old company. He claimed he was to have received $30 a head for every one who *had life in him*, that was landed, independent of his condition, even though he might die before he could be housed. Such was not the contract.

Imagine the scene portrayed by this letter. There on the banks of Jekyl Island lay the negroes, dying because of the torments they had endured, while Lamar and the captain stood by quarrelling over the blood money.

In the record of the meetings of the New York Yacht Club for 1859 (a thin little 12mo manuscript volume) can be found, under the date of February 3, a preamble and resolutions expelling Corrie from the club and erasing the name of the *Wanderer* from the club's squadron list. The club did this not only because Corrie had violated the law, "but more especially from his being engaged in a traffic repugnant to humanity and to the moral sense of the members of this association."

There were many slavers living in New York then, but they were not considered fit for membership in the New York Yacht Club.

According to Lamar's letter-book, the *Wanderer* was stolen out of Savannah, after the second voyage to Africa, by a Captain D. S. Martin. "He has undoubtedly gone to the coast of Africa for a cargo of negroes," says Lamar; "and if he is as smart there as he has been here, he will get one."

The *Wanderer* was eventually captured by the Federal forces, and was, for a time, used as revenue cutter at Pensacola. Then she was sold at auction and was put into the cocoanut trade by a firm dealing with the islands on the north coast of Honduras, and there she remained until driven ashore on Cape

Henry, where her bones found a last resting-place.
Lamar was killed in battle during the civil war.

One might tell in considerable detail, too, the story
of the slaver *Clotilde*, a schooner of three hundred
and twenty-seven tons built by Captain Timothy
Meagher on the Mobile River late in the fall of 1858.
Timothy bought one hundred and seventy-five prime
slaves in Africa, and landed them without the loss of
one (a most humane voyage) near Mobile City.   But it
did not pay.   The negroes cost too much ($8,640 gold,
besides ninety cases of rum and eight cases of cloths),
and only twenty-five could be sold, because of the
discovery of the importation and the rush of officials
for prize money.   The Captain sunk in all nearly
$100,000.

As to the extent of the smuggling Stephen A.
Douglas said in public that he believed 15,000 slaves
were smuggled into the United States in 1859.   A
correspondent wrote to the *Tribune* in 1860 that
"twelve vessels will discharge their living freight
upon our shores within ninety days from the 1st of
June last."   Douglas's position on the slaver question cost him dearly—he failed of election as President because of it.

In spite of a pretence of prosecuting the slavers detected in their work, the Government in those days
practically aided them by failing to prosecute them to
conviction for the crime committed.   Out of sixty
persons arrested as slavers, "who have been bailed
from the first day of May, 1852, to the first day of
May, 1862," says a report made by Secretary of the
Interior Caleb B. Smith, the following disposition had
been made : Eight cases were still pending; nine had

been tried and acquitted by the jury; no bill had been found in two cases; in one case "Defendant could not be found, but the bond was not forfeited"; in another, "Defendant surrendered his bail, but afterward escaped." In all other instances the case was dismissed or a nolle was entered.

In one of Lamar's letters was a reference to what he calls his missionary work, and that is a subject needing further notice. An examination of newspapers and periodicals shows that many slave-owners had a strong desire for the expansion of the slave territory. Filibustering expeditions like that of Walker to Nicaragua grew out of it. Pollard in his "Black Diamonds" speaks of Walker as one of a number of men who looked over the whole territory bordering on the Caribbean Sea and the Gulf of Mexico as a vast field for slave-holders to acquire in order that they might make of it a slave empire that should supply the world with cotton, coffee, sugar, and other staples, all to be produced by slave labor for the benefit of the dominant race. Pollard called the dream magnificent.

Then there was the plan for buying Cuba which Buchanan aided, as already mentioned. Spain could have had $100,000,000 for the island then.

In addition to these evidences of restlessness were the efforts made to reopen the slave-trade between Africa and the United States.

In *De Bow's* for November, 1858, is the following:

"It cannot be denied that the Southern States—more especially those in which are grown the great staples of cotton, sugar, and rice—demand a greater number of negro laborers than can now possibly be acquired by natural increase or from those home sources which have hitherto yielded but a sparse supply."

The price of slaves was increasing rapidly, the writer continues. Quotations from reports of auction sales showed that " the price has already reached that point which is beyond the means of small planters." Able men sold as high as $1,835 cash. The lowest price for an adult at a sale quoted was "Olivia, $1,-140." There was, of course, but one remedy—the reopening of the African slave-trade.

This is a fair sample of many similar appeals in periodicals. Pamphlets were printed and circulated. One of them made a most potent appeal to all the merchants and manufacturers having trade with slave-owners. The character of the appeal appears from its title, "Southern Wealth and Northern Profits." It may be found in the libraries.

Meantime conventions were called wherein orators could proclaim views which were, of course, printed afterward in the newspapers. It was "a campaign of education."

For instance, there was the convention of May 10, 1858, held at Montgomery, Ala. Spratt, of South Carolina, from the committee on the slave-trade, introduced the following resolutions (quoted in Du Bois):

"*Resolved*, That slavery is right, and that, being right, there can be no wrong in the natural means to its formation.

"*Resolved*, That it is expedient and proper that the foreign slave-trade should be reopened, and that this convention will lend its influence to any legitimate measure to that end."

When some of the more conservative men present mildly objected, Yancey declared that "if it is right

to buy slaves in Virginia and carry them to New Orleans, why is it not right to buy them in Cuba, Brazil,
or Africa, and carry them there?"

His question was, of course, unanswerable. He
might also have said that if it was right to *own*
negroes it was right to buy them wherever they were
on sale and take them to any place where they were
needed. Although he did not know it, he was clearing the much-befogged road leading to the point of
view from which might be seen the real evil principle
at the bottom of slavery.

At Vicksburg, in 1859, a convention of commercial
men resolved by a vote of forty to nineteen that "all
laws, State or Federal, prohibiting the African slave-
trade ought to be repealed;" also that "the convention raise a fund to be dispensed in premiums for the
best sermons in favor of reopening the African Slave-
trade!"

The reopening of the trade was also advocated on
the floor of Congress. Omitting many quotations
that might be made from the words of slave-holding
Congressmen it will be sufficient to note what two
who were representative of their class said. Alexander Stephens, in his farewell address to his constituents, according to reputable reports, used these
words: "Slave-States cannot be made without Africans. . . . [My object is] to bring clearly to your
mind the great truth that without an increase of African slaves from abroad you may not expect or look
for many more slave-States."

Jefferson Davis, while opposing an immediate reopening of the trade, denied "any coincidence of opinion
with those who prate of the inhumanity and sinful-

ness of the trade. The interest of Mississippi, not of the African, dictates my conclusion.'' He thought to open the trade immediately would flood Mississippi with negroes by bringing in more than could be profitably and safely handled, but '' this conclusion, in relation to Mississippi, is based upon my view of her *present* condition, *not* upon any *general theory.* It is not supposed to be applicable to Texas, to New Mexico, or to any *future acquisitions* to be made south of the Rio Grande.''

But the rising tide of the power of those who believed in human slavery had reached its highest level. While slave-holders were holding conventions in which to advocate the reopening of the slave-trade, the abolitionists were in a thousand ways proclaiming the right of every human being to life, liberty, and the pursuit of happiness. A few were even proclaiming the strange doctrine that the superior race, instead of having, by virtue of its superiority, the right to oppress the weak, was, by the example and command of Almighty God, bound to uplift and carry the burden of the weak. A river of Jordan running bankful of blood lay before us, and we were about to bathe in it and be healed.

CHAPTER XX

WHEN THE END CAME

Buchanan's Administration and the Slave-trade—When the Sham Efforts to Suppress Came to an End—Story of Captain Gordon of the *Erie,* the First Slaver Pirate to be Executed in the United States.

As hitherto noted, the slave-trade differed from all other kinds of traffic known to the history of the world. In every other traffic there was (and there is) a steady amelioration of the condition of all persons engaged in it. The African slave-trade to the Americas began with the work of a good bishop who saw that it was more humane to enslave the hardy African than the effeminate red aborigines. From that the trade descended to a level where it was, for that day, an ordinary commercial enterprise, and then, because it was profitable and was becoming steadily more profitable, it reached out to overwhelm with its suffering, as well as its shame, not only everyone connected with it, whether directly or indirectly, but it drenched with its sorrows uncounted thousands who had never had any part in it, and still other thousands who had opposed it.

But even while Buchanan was striving to buy Cuba on the pretence that thus the slave-trade would be suppressed, the end of America's shame was at hand.

It was not in the blood of the race to perpetuate hypocrisy and injustice forever.

Those of us who are old enough recall with strange feelings the tumultuous controversies of the days of the Buchanan Administration. The pelting of words was incessant, but back of all that and growing steadily more ominous, was the tornado roar of one mighty question, Shall the Right prevail in the United States of America ?

Granville Sharp, as the friend of one oppressed negro, had asked that question, standing alone, in other years. Now tens of thousands of the mightiest, most heroic souls of the earth were standing up to answer it, not by words alone but by freely giving their life blood.

Yet let no injustice be done now in recalling that controversy. As long as a people "holds its life in its hand, ready to give it for its honor (though a foolish honor) ; for its love (though a foolish love) ; for its business (though a foolish business), there is hope for it." The slave-owners, too, held their lives in their hands. No higher proof of their sincerity is known to man. Nathan Hale, whose statue stands in the City Hall Park of New York, reached out both hands (albeit with sorrow) when he welcomed to the further shore the spirits of those Americans who cheerfully went to their death in the *David* torpedo-boat, of Charleston harbor. We were to determine not only whether the right should prevail, but to see what was right, and our pool of Siloam was full to the brim of blood.

But when that is said—when the entire sincerity of the masses of those who sought to perpetuate slavery is proclaimed—the fact remains (and we can all see it now) that our Declaration of Independence had been for three-quarters of a century a grinning mask. It could not remain so longer. The spirit that had inspired the men who made that Declaration, not fully knowing what they did, was ready at last to turn the mask into the flushed face of the goddess of America. A time had come when a President who could understand the immortal words was to be elected, and he was elected. The laws against the slave-trade were now to be executed. The spirit of the Declaration of Independence was now not only to be enacted in statutes, but, within limits, to become the faith of the people.

Under Buchanan it was possible for the slave-bark *Cora* to be captured on the coast of Africa on the 18th day of May, carried to New York, let go after a form of condemnation, and then captured once more on the slave-coast, on December 10 of the same year.

With the advent of Abraham Lincoln the sham passed away. Here was a man who had the first characteristics of all heroes—sincerity and strength. He would, with charity for all and with malice toward none, and with such obstacles in his way as no American had ever faced before, and no American will ever face again—he would do his duty. Of all books that have been written here and may now be had for a price, there is none so well worth the study of an American reader, if he will but seek the heart of it, as a Life of Abraham Lincoln. But the American Carlyle has yet to come to place the heart of it plainly before us.

In a letter regarding the slave-trade written by Mr.

Seward to Lord Lyons, on March 22, 1862, it is said that the last slave-smuggler was the *Wanderer*, already described. Possibly—in fact, very likely—small parties were brought over from Cuba after she landed her cargo, but she was the last regular slave-ship to come to our coasts.

The blockade of the Confederate ports by the Federal ships, however, in 1861 ended all slave-smuggling here. Nevertheless the smuggling of slaves into the Spanish colonies in America was carried on for a long time after our civil war ended. The trade is called smuggling because during all the weary years after 1820—the weary years during which so many negroes were thrown overboard that every wave of the sea in the Middle Passage became a mound over a body that had been tortured to death—during all those years the laws of Spain prohibited the traffic. Mr. Seward, in view of the fact "that this infamous traffic has been carried on by persons resident in other countries, including the United States," was prepared to open negotiations for a convention with Her Majesty's Government that should be worthy of the civilizations of the age. The shams of previous administrations, and the clap-trap about the right of search and the sacredness of our flag, were to come to an end, and they did end in a treaty that was concluded at Washington on April 7, 1862. To give it effect, Congress made two appropriations of $900,000 each. The days when an American cruiser, out of fifteen months' service in the African squadron, would spend no more than fifteen days on the slave-coast, as really happened under the sham, were now at an end. The days when American naval officers were to go

through the forms of executing the laws, while hampered by the Department, were also at an end. There were, indeed, slavers afloat thereafter. While the market existed, and such enormous profits were to be made, even the severest measures could, perhaps, but repress. By a treaty made with Great Britain on February 17, 1863, the limits of the territory wherein the mutual right of search existed were greatly extended. Even as late as 1870, Great Britain and the United States had to strengthen still further their agreement for the suppression of the trade, because a few slavers were yet on the high seas. It was not until about 1886 that the Spaniards (and some American citizens) ceased to own slaves in Cuba, but the slave-trade began its death throes—it for the first time felt a real strangling pressure on its throat—when this treaty was made.

Detailed stories of some of the slavers owned in New York but trading to Cuba are to be had by the student in sufficient number. For instance, George Howe, M.D., told the story of his experience in "The Last Slave-Ship," in *Scribner's Magazine* for July, 1890. The story of how Appleton Oaksmith, written also Oaks Smith), the son of an honored poetess, disgraced his name by trying to get away for a slaver voyage in the whaler bark *Augusta* is told in Government documents. This is a particularly interesting story from the fact that Oaksmith was prosecuted by Mr. Stewart L. Woodford, late United States Minister to Spain, then just beginning his public career by serving as an assistant to the United States District Attorney in New York City. It brings the slave-trade close down to the present day, so to speak, when we remember that the well-known diplomat of 1898 began his public career by prosecuting a slaver. But all of these stories must be omitted in order to emphasize that of a slaver whose fate marked the end of the heinious traffic.

In the summer of 1860, Captain Nathaniel Gordon, of the ship *Erie*, took his vessel to Havana and there completed an outfit for the slave-trade that he had begun buying in New York. Gordon was a citizen of Portland, Me., and had made already, it was said, three slave voyages. On leaving Havana he went directly to the Congo River, and sailed forty-five miles up into the interior. There he discharged a cargo of liquor, and having prepared his ship for her return cargo of slaves he came down near the mouth of the stream, where on the afternoon of August 7, 1860, he brought on board the slaves, and "thrust them, densely crowded, between the decks, and immediately set sail for Cuba." The slaves numbered eight hundred and ninety, of whom but one hundred and seventy-two were men. The women numbered one hundred and six, and the remainder were boys and girls. Gordon was one of those slavers who carried children because it was safer to carry them. They would but flinch and scream when he tortured them; they would never strike back.

As it happened the United States warship *Mohican* was fifty miles off shore next morning, and the *Erie*, while crowding sail for Havana, was seen and captured. The negroes were taken to Liberia and landed, while the *Erie* and Gordon were sent to New York for trial. The ship was soon disposed of. She had been taken with the slaves on board, and even in 1860 she was sure to be condemned, because the condemnation would bring considerable sums of money to all concerned in her capture and condemnation. She was sold, on October 4th of the same year, at auction, for $7,823.25, showing she was a right good ship, for she measured but five hundred tons.

To punish Gordon as a pirate under the law of 1820 was another matter, and when he was first brought to face the charge there was a mistrial. But in the meantime a new administration had come in, and a District Attorney, E. Delafield Smith, who respected his oath of office, had been appointed.

Gordon was once more put on trial on November 6, 1861. He was defended by ex-Judge Dean and P. J. Joachimson, who were experienced in such cases. Judge Nelson presided. In two hours a jury was obtained.

The papers of that day say that but few spectators were in court during the trial. The public showed very little interest in the case. The Civil War was in progress, and how could anyone stop to consider the trial of a ship captain who had been on trial once before, had secured a disagreement of the jury, and, if precedent counted for anything, was likely to go free in the end? Even the most sensational papers of the day gave the trial but scanty space. So, with never a thought that they were making important history, the Judge and the lawyers and the jury worked away. The plea, as was usual in such cases, was that Gordon was a passenger, having turned the command over to a foreigner carried along for the purpose. On the afternoon of Friday, November 8, the attorneys ended their part of the trial, Judge Nelson delivered his charge, and at 7 o'clock in the evening the jury retired. Twenty minutes later they came back with the verdict.

"Guilty."

"Gordon heard the verdict without emotion," so the reporters described the scene, and they were about the only spectators outside of those directly interested in the case.

But when that verdict had appeared in print, next day, the people of New York woke up to the importance of what had occurred. On Saturday, November 30, when motions for a new trial had been denied, and Gordon was commanded to stand up and hear his doom, he arose to his feet in a court-room "densely packed" with people who had come to hear the sentence of the first American slaver convicted as a pirate.

As Gordon heard the command to stand up his face changed color rapidly, but once on his feet he recovered his composure, and in reply to the usual question said, with a forced smile,

"I have nothing to say whatever."

At that Judge Nelson began to speak. He recited the facts in the case, warned the prisoner that as he had shown no mercy to the unfortunate he could expect none now from the Court, and ended by ordering that the slaver be, on February 7, 1862, between the hours of noon and three in the afternoon, hanged by the neck until he was dead.

When February 7 came Gordon had been respited for two weeks by the President. "It was currently reported that the President had commuted the sentence," said one paper, but Marshal Murray knew better, and when Gordon looked in his face, on receiving the respite, he saw his fate.

"Mr. Marshal, then there is no hope?" he asked.

"Not the slightest," replied Murray.

There was no lack of effort, however, to save the pirate. Even on the last day of his life, one of his attorneys telegraphed that the Governor of the State had appealed to the President, and asked for a delay for a reply, but Murray explained that an arrangement had been concluded with the President by which no telegram from any source whatever should interfere.

Nor was that all that was done to save him. Threats were made that a rescuing mob to storm the jail would be raised—threats that were really ominous, for that was a day when innocent negroes were hanged to lamp-posts by a New York mob.

But a guard of eighty marines from the navy-yard filed into the yard of the city prison on the morning of February 21, 1862, and there loaded their muskets with ball cartridges, and fixed their bayonets. And that ended the possibility of mob attacks.

Meantime Gordon had passed the early part of the night in writing letters. At one o'clock in the morning he went to sleep and slept for two hours. On waking he managed to swallow a dose of strychnine he had obtained for the occasion. As it began to work he gnashed his teeth at the guards and shouted,

"I've cheated you! I've cheated you!"

But he was mistaken, for physicians saved him alive and conscious for the gallows. Two or three notes were written by him after his recovery from the poison, and then, just before the noon hour, the Marshal came to the cell and in the usual course read the death warrant and asked Gordon if he had anything to say.

For a moment the prisoner was silent, and then in a firm voice he replied :

"My conscience is clear. I have no fault to find with the treatment I have received from the Marshal and his Deputy, Mr. Thompson ; but any public man who will get up in open court and say to the jury, 'If you convict this prisoner, I will be the first man to sign a petition for his pardon,' and will then go to the Executive to prevent his commuting the sentence, is a man who will do anything to promote his own ends, I do not care what people may say.'

It was a remarkable speech to make in the shadow of the gallows, for the charge it contained against District Attorney Smith was untrue. The reporters hunted up the stenographic report of the speech to the jury and found no such words in it.

At noon, on February 21, 1862, Nathaniel Gordon, with a slanderous lie on his lips, started for the gallows. "He was deathly pale with terror [says the New York *Tribune* of February 22, 1862], his head hung over his shoulder, and his limbs almost refused their office. He tottered as he stood beneath the fatal beam, [so that] he had to be supported. At a given signal the cord was snapped asunder by the executioner's axe and Nathaniel Gordon was hoisted aloft into mid-air. A few convulsive twitches of the body followed. The veins of his neck and hands swelled and stood out hard ; then the limbs lost their rigidity, the flesh assumed a livid hue, and the slave-trader, now a lump of dishonored clay, swung slowly to and fro in the frosty air."

For more than three hundred years the oppressed had been crying from the foul hold of the slaver, "How long, O Lord, how long?" But when the axe fell, and the rope creaked to the weight of that dishonored clay, the sweet angel of Mercy was at last able to reply:

"Now."

APPENDIX A.

FROM SEN. EX. DOC. 53, 37TH CONG., 2D SESS.

Names and number of vessels arrested and bonded from the first day of May, 1852, to the first day of May, 1862, in the Southern District of New York, charged with being engaged in the slave-trade, together with the names of the bondsmen, the amounts they were bonded for, and the amounts realized by the Government.

Names of Vessels.	Where Arrested.	When Libelled.	When Bonded.	Names of Bondsmen.	Amount Bonded for.	Disposition of Case, and Amount Realized on Forfeiture.
Sch. *George H. Townsend*	....	Dec., 1854.	Dec. 29, 1854.	T. W. Hutchinson..........	$5,000 00	Libel dismissed.
Sch. *Falmouth* and cargo.....	....	March 18, 1856.	....	....	....	Condemned and sold for $5,000.
Sch. *Onward*....	....	January 31, 1855.	....	....	....	Never arrested.
Brig *Braman*....	Coast of Africa.	June 9, 1856.	June 18, 1856.*	Sovereigns bonded by José B. da Cunha, B. da Cunha Reiz, Henry M. Barnes, and M. B da Cunha Reiz. Vessel bonded by Manuel J. Frazer, by J. Braddick, Attorney, Thos. J. G. Blumersrother, and John Levi. Cargo bonded by Patrick McGrary and Henriques da Costa.	£217 £61½ †$6,200 00 ‡ 857 95	Case still pending.

* Money found on board bonded ; September 16, 1856, vessel bonded ; November 1, 1856, cargo bonded.　　† Vessel.　　‡ Cargo.

15

Names of Vessels.	Where Arrested.	When Libelled.	When Bonded.	Names of Bondsmen.	Amount Bonded for.	Disposition of Case, and Amount Realized on Forfeiture.
Bark Orion.....	Coast of Africa.	June 21, 1859.	August 6. 1859.	Rudolph Blumenberg and H. S. Vining for vessel; Rudolph Blumenberg and J. F. D. Miranda for cargo.	*$12,000 00 † 5,923 95	Condemned, execution returned nulla bona. Blumenberg's conviction for perjury in justification as bail, recently procured by United States district attorney; State prison five years.
Bark Ardennes and cargo.....	Coast of Africa.	June 30, 1859.	Sept. 20, 1859.	Horace F. Parish and Merrit N. Craft.	7,029 68	Case still pending.
Brig J. P. Hooper.....		Nov. 1, 1859.		(Vessel remained in custody)....		Libel dismissed, May 2, 1860.
Ship Emily and cargo.........	Coast of Africa.	Nov. 15, 1859.	January 14, 1860.	Wm. M. Arnold and Stephen Kelly.	4,776 80	Case still pending.
Bark Charlotte E. Tay and cargo.........	New York.	April 24, 1860.	May 10, 1860.	Jesse A. Braddock and Fred K. Myer.	6,354 71	Case still pending.
Bark Cora and cargo.....	New York.	May 18, 1860.	June 23, 1860.	Robert Griffiths and Chas. Newman.	22,128 33	Condemned and execution issued; returned nulla bona.
Sch. Josephene and cargo.....	New York.	May 28, 1860.	June 22, 1860.	David Decker and Benjamin Isaacs.	12,174 59	Case still pending.
Brig Falmouth and cargo.....	Coast of Africa.	June 18, 1860.				Sold as perishable property for $1,058.32, and amount paid into court; case still pending as to $272, amount of proceeds above costs and sailors' wages.

Vessel						
Sch. *Mariquita* and cargo.....	New York.	June 16, 1860.	July 10, 1860.	James E. Ward, James A. Van Brunt, Michael Rupp, Pierre L. Pierce, Henry M. Barnes and H. C. Lyon.	24,500 00	Libel dismissed January 28, 1851.
Brig *Thomas Achorn*......	Coast of Africa.	Aug. 16, 1860.	December 4, 1860.	Joseph Santos and George H. Blanchard.	3,485 00	Case still pending.
Bark *Kate* and cargo.........	New York.	July 6, 1860.	August 30, 1860.	John J. Diehl......	9,300 00	Case still pending.
Brig *W. R. Kibby*........	Coast of Cuba.	August 4, 1860.	....	....	....	Condemned and sold for $4,551.47.
Bark *Weather-gage*.........	New York.	October 1, 1860.	....	(Still in custody)............	....	Condemned and argued on appeal, and awaiting decision of the court.
Ship *Erie*.........	Coast of Africa.	October 4, 1860.	....	....	....	Condemned and sold for $7,823.25.
Sch. *William J. Cogswell*......	New York.	Nov. 28, 1860.	....	(Vessel remained in custody)	....	February 4, 1861, libel dismissed.
Bark *Cora* and cargo......	Coast of Africa.	Dec. 10, 1860.	....	....	....	Condemned and sold for $9,596.62.
Bark *Sarah* and cargo......	New York.	April 6, 1861.	Feb. 2, 1862.	Joseph W. Yates and Robert Porterfield.	16,886 21	Condemned and argued on appeal, and awaiting decision of the court.
Ship *Nightin-gale*.........	Coast of Africa.	June 20, 1861.	....	....	....	Condemned and sold for $13,501.10.
Bark *Augusta* and cargo......	Greenport, L. I.	June 19, 1861.	October 28, 1861.	Isaac Peck and Joseph Wagler..	4,250 00	Condemned and case pending on appeal.

* Vessel.   † Cargo.

Names of Vessels.	Where Arrested.	When Libelled.	When Bonded.	Names of Bondsmen.	Amount Bonded for.	Disposition of Case, and Amount Realized on Forfeiture.
Brig *Fulmouth* and cargo.....	Coast of Africa.	August 2, 1861.	October 1, 1861.	George H. Leinas and William Watts.	$1,665 00	Case still pending.
Brig *Triton* and cargo....	Coast of Africa.	July 12, 1861.	August 6, 1861.*	Peyton A. Key, John S. Pearson and J. A. Leland.	2,379 00	Case still pending.
Bark *Agusta*.....	Greenport, L. I.	Nov. 11, 1861.		(Still in custody).............	....	Case still pending.

* Vessel bonded : September 2, 1861, cargo bonded.
It should be observed that vessels were more readily condemned in our courts than men were because "there was money in it," when vessels were condemned—fees and bounties for officials and informers.

APPENDIX B.

From Sen. Ex. Doc. 53, 37th Cong., 2d Sess.

Names of all persons arrested who have been bailed from the first day of May, 1852, to the first day of May, 1862, in the Southern District of New York, charged with being engaged in the slave-trade, together with the names of the bondsmen, the amounts of the bonds, and the amounts the Government has realized from the forfeiture thereof.

Names.	When Arrested.	When Bailed.	Names of Bondsmen.	Amount of Bonds.	Disposition of the Cases, and Amounts Realized on Forfeitures.
Manuel Echeverria..	June, 1855.	Sept. 25, 1855.	Andrew Patrullo and Francisco del Hoyo.	$20,000	Bond not forfeited, defendant tried and acquitted.
Stephen E. Glover ..	Oct., 1854.	April, 25, 1855,	John J. Boyd and Joseph McMurray.	20,000	Bond not forfeited, no bill being found by grand jury.
Jeronimo Hermes ...	June, 1855.	June 29, 1855.	John A. Machado..........	10,000	Bond not forfeited; complaint dismissed.
L. Kraft *alias* G. Filetti............	Jan., 1855.	Jan. 29, 1855.	George Van Staveren and Ramon Palanca.	5,000	Bond not forfeited; complaint dismissed.
William F. Martin..	May, 1855.	July 14, 1855.	Philo V. Beebee............	2,500	Bond not forfeited; tried and acquitted.
Theodore A. Myers..	May, 1855.	May 26, 1855.	Robert J. Walker, A. C. Washington, C. H. Ring.	5,000	Bond not forfeited; tried and acquitted.
Bartholomew Blanco.	Oct., 1854.	Oct. 11, 1854.	Edward Baulker and Charles G. Staffani.	20,000	Bond not forfeited; no bill found.
William C. Valentine..	Sept. 20, 1854.	Sept. 20, 1854.	David T. Valentine, Bassett B. Boerum, and James S. Libby.	20,000	Bond not forfeited; defendant tried and acquitted.

Names.	When Arrested.	When Bailed.	Names of Bondsmen.	Amount of Bonds.	Disposition of the Cases, and Amounts Realized on Forfeitures.
Jasper M. Da Cunha.	April, 1857.	June 5, 1858.	George M. Rea............	$2,500	Bond not forfeited; *nolle prosequi* entered, 1858.
Placido de Castro...	June, 1856.	July 17, 1856.	José Varoni............	2,500	Bond not forfeited; defendant tried and acquitted.
Rudolph E. Lasala..	May, 1855.	Nov. 14, 1855.	Nicholas Del Rio, Daniel Curtis.	7,500	Bond not forfeited; defendant tried and acquitted.
Philip S. Van Vechten.	May, 1857.	May 2, 1857.	Junnis R. Van Vechten and John P. Weeks.	5,000	Bond not forfeited; complaint dismissed.
J. De Aranga......	May, 1857.	May 2, 1857.	Peter Gilsey and Edwin P. Christy.	5,000	Bond not forfeited; complaint dismissed.
Lewis Pulver......	May, 1857.	May 25, 1857.	Edwin R. Kirk........	5,000	Bond not forfeited.
John Jones........	May, 1857.	May 27, 1857.	Jesse A. Braddick......	500	Bond not forfeited.
Lenia Vianna......	Oct., 1857.	Oct. 26, 1857.	Zopher Pearsall........	10,000	Bond not forfeited; *nolle prosequi* 1858.
José Santos........	April, 1857.	Oct. 26, 1857,	Jesse A. Braddick......	2,000	Bond not forfeited; *nolle prosequi* entered, 1858.
Jos. A. Yates......	1857.	July 21, 1857.	Joseph W. Yates........	1,000	Bond not forfeited.
Benj. F. Wenberg...	Oct., 1856.	Oct. 22, 1857.	Horace J. Moody........	2,000	Bond not forfeited; tried and acquitted.
Juan M. Smith.....	Oct., 1857.	Oct. 22, 1857.	Robert Porterfield and H. M. Barnes.	2,000	Bond not forfeited; *nolle prosequi* entered, 1858.
Basilio La Cunha Reis........	June, 1856.	June 26, 1856.	George W. Roosevelt and G. J. De La Figaniere.	5,000	Bond not forfeited; tried and acquitted.
Placido de Castro ...	June, 1856.	June 26, 1856.	Joseph Varona........	2,500	Bond not forfeited; tried and acquitted.
Henrico de Costa....	June, 1856.	June 21, 1856.	Henry M. Barnes........	5,000	Defendant surrendered by his bail, and afterward escaped.
Augusta C. de Mesquite........	Oct., 1856.	Nov. 11, 1851.	Geo. M. Rea and John Radway, jr.	5,000	Bond not forfeited; tried and acquitted.

Name					Disposition
Benj. F. Wenberg...	Oct., 1856.	Nov. 6, 1856.	Thomas A. Gerry and Jacob R. Telfair.	5,000	Bond not forfeited; tried and acquitted.
John P. Weeks. ...	Oct., 1856.	Nov. 6, 1856.	Benj. Newhouse............	....	Bond not forfeited; tried and acquitted.
Wm. C. Stewart.....	June, 1859.	June 16, 1859.	Thos. Collins.............	250	Bond not forfeited; complaint dismissed.
John Williams.......	June, 1859.	June 16, 1859.	Jesse A. Bradick..........	250	Bond not forfeited; complaint dismissed.
Jos. Williams........	June, 1859.	June 16, 1859.	Jesse A. Bradick..........	250	Bond not forfeited; complaint dismissed.
Henry Williams......	June, 1859.	June 16, 1859.	Jesse A. Bradick..........	250	Bond not forfeited; complaint dismissed.
Richard Welch.......	June, 1859.	June 16, 1859.	Thomas Collins	250	Bond not forfeited; complaint dismissed.
Thomas Morgan.....	June, 1859.	June 16, 1859.	Jesse A. Bradick..........	1,000	Bond not forfeited; complaint dismissed.
George Paul.	June, 1859.	June 16, 1859.	Jesse A. Bradick..........	250	Bond not forfeited; complaint dismissed.
William Fisher	June, 1859.	June 16, 1859.	Jesse A. Bradick..........	250	Bond not forfeited; complaint dismissed.
Robert Horn........	June, 1859.	June 16, 1859.	Jesse A. Bradick..........	250	Bond not forfeited; complaint dismissed.
Harmon Beeker......	June, 1859.	June 16, 1859.	Jesse A. Bradick..........	250	Bond not forfeited; complaint dismissed.
Jonathan Brown.....	June, 1859.	June 16, 1859.	Jesse A. Bradick..........	250	Bond not forfeited; complaint dismissed.
Tristas P. Conhoo...	June, 1859.	June 16, 1859.	Jesse A. Bradick..........	1,000	Bond not forfeited; complaint dismissed.
Thos. Carolton......	June, 1859.	June 16, 1859.	Jesse A. Bradick..........	250	Bond not forfeited; complaint dismissed.
Wm. C. Carter......	May, 1860.	May 20, 1860.	John J. Diehl.............	3,000	Defendant was indicted June 25, 1860, and could not be found; but the bond was not forfeited.
John A. Machado...	Aug., 1861.	Sept. 11, 1861.	George A. Vogel...........	5,000	Bond not forfeited; complaint being dismissed.
Wm. Pratt.........	April, 1861.	July 27, 1861.	Charles M. Terry.........	1,000	Bond not forfeited, no bill being found.
Antonio Orse	Dec., 1860.	May 3, 1861.	John F. Broderick........	500	Bond not forfeited, *nolle prosequi* being entered.

Names.	When Arrested.	When Bailed.	Names of Bondsmen.	Amount of Bonds.	Disposition of the Cases, and Amounts Realized on Forfeitures.
Nathaniel Currier...	Dec., 1860.	May 3, 1861.	John F. Broderick..........	$500	Bond not forfeited, *nolle prosequi* being entered.
José Sanchez	Dec., 1860.	May 3, 1861.	John F. Broderick..........	500	Bond not forfeited, *nolle prosequi* being entered.
Manuel St. Savara..	Dec., 1860.	Feb. 21, 1861.	Garrett Erkson	500	Bond not forfeited, *nolle prosequi* being entered.
Sidney Oaksmith ...	Nov., 1861.	Nov. 20, 1861.	Orvin D. Case.............	500	Bond not forfeited; complaint being dismissed.
Walter R. Haven....	Nov., 1861.	Nov. 20, 1861.	Orvin D. Case.............	500	Bond not forfeited ; complaint being dismissed.
Bartolo Grau	Dec., 1860.	Oct. 8, 1861.	Alex. Melville..............	500	Bond not forfeited; *nolle prosequi* being entered.
Erastus H. Booth...	Sept., 1861.	March 24, 1862.	Pliny S. Mills.............	2,000	Case still pending.
Erastus H. Booth...	Sept., 1861.	Feb. 27, 1862.	Wm. Albatson and Benj. Wells.	3,000	Case still pending.
Joseph E. Santos	August, 1861.	Aug. 14, 1861.	James Murphy....	5,000	Case still pending.
Albert Horn.........	April, 1861.	Aug. 13, 1861.	W. R. Beebe and Guy R. Pelton.	5,000	Case still pending.
Minthurne Wester- velt.	June, 1861.	Nov. 25, 1861.	John S. Westervelt and Francis Man.	5,000	Case still pending.
Frederick Otto......	July, 1860.	July 10, 1860.	Jesse A. Braddick..........	1,500	Bond forfeited, and suit commenced; suit still pending.
Henrico Da Costa...	July, 1860.	Sept. 18, 1860.	Philo V. Beebe.............	5,000	Bond forfeited, and suit commenced; suit still pending.
George H. Lienas ...	Sept., 1861.	Sept. 19, 1861.	W. R. Beebe...............	2,000	Bond not forfeited ; complaint dismissed.
Alberti Givins......	Nov., 1861.	Nov. 22, 1861.	W. R. Beebe...............	500	Bond not forfeited ; complaint dismissed.
J. M. Smith........	Feb., 1862.	Feb. 10, 1862.	C. Donohue.............	3,000	Case still pending.
Albert Horn.........	April, 1861.	May 4, 1861.	W. R. Beebe and Guy R. Pelton.	5,000	Case still pending.
Pierre L. Pierce.....	Sept., 1860.	Oct. 6, 1860.	Ward A. Work.............	5,000	Bond not forfeited ; *nolle prosequi* entered.